A COMPREHENSIVE COURSE IN TWI

A COMPREHENSIVE COURSE IN TWI (ASANTE) FOR THE NON-TWI LEARNER

FLORENCE ABENA DOLPHYNE
Associate Professor, Department of Linguistics
University of Ghana, Legon.

GHANA UNIVERSITIES PRESS
ACCRA
1996

Ghana Universities Press
P. O. Box GP 4219
Accra

Produced in Ghana
Typesetting by Florence Abena Dolphyne
Printing and binding by Assemblies of God Literature Centre
Limited, Accra.

CONTENTS

PREFACE

Asante Twi is the most widely spoken of the dialects of the Akan language. Akan is spoken by about 44 percent of Ghana's population as a first language by people living in the Ashanti Region and in parts of the Eastern, Western, Central, Volta and Brong Ahafo Regions of the country. On account of its central geographical location among the dialects of Akan, Asante Twi is easily understood by speakers of the other Akan dialects. It is one of the three literary dialects of Akan, the others being Akuapem Twi, spoken in parts of the Eastern Region, and Fante, spoken in the Central and parts of the Western Regions of Ghana.

This book is meant to introduce a non-Twi beginner to the spoken language. It may also be used by someone who has some knowledge of the language, but who wants to improve his/her competence in it, because it contains a section on the grammar of the language and also has a considerable English-Twi vocabulary.

The book may be used with or without an instructor. It comes with a tape recording of the Twi texts, and the learner is advised to listen to them as often as is necessary to get, especially, the intonation right. If used with an instructor, the instructor should first read through the dialogue, sentence by sentence, and have the learner(s) repeat each sentence, making sure that the pronunciation, especially the intonation, is as close to a native speaker's as possible. The instructor should then read the part of one speaker and let a student read the part of the other speaker. After this the instructor reverses roles and does the dialogue with the same or a different student. This should be done as often as is necessary until the student can say the sentences with some fluency.

Although the lessons are not strictly graded, that is, with each subsequent lesson being more difficult than the preceding one, it is recommended that the lessons in Part I should be studied in the order in which they are presented in the book.

The book is divided into two parts: Part I introduces the learner to the language, with dialogues based on everyday encounters with people. Part II discusses, in a systematic way, aspects of the grammar of the language. These are also illustrated with appropriate dialogues. In addition, there are appendices that deal with idiomatic expressions and some aspects of the culture of the speakers of the language. It also provides a selection of literary works that the advanced learner may read to improve his/her competence in the language, as well as a limited English-Twi vocabulary.

Every effort has been made to ensure that the dialogues are as natural and as close to current everyday usage as possible, so that expressions such as 'Auntie Amma' and 'Brother Kofi' are used, even though some people may argue that 'Auntie' and 'Brother' are not Twi words. Where the pronunciation of a word or an expression is considerably different from the written form, the pronunciation is indicated the first few times the item occurs by enclosing it in square brackets, as in *merekɔ* [meekɔ] 'I'm going'.

The main focus of this course is the **spoken** language, and so common expressions such as *Mepa wo kyɛw*: 'Please'; *Meda wo ase*: 'Thank you'; and everyday greetings such as *Me ma wo akyē* : 'Good morning', are consistently presented in the text as *Mepaakyɛw, Medaase* and *Maakyē*.

A limited vocabulary is introduced in each new dialogue. The new words are listed at the end of the dialogue. Every effort should be made to learn these words, and to make up new sentences with them. It may be advisable to keep a notebook, and to write down the new words as they come up in each lesson. Where the vocabulary item is borrowed from English, the word is written the way it is pronounced in Twi. For names, however, the English spelling is retained.

Aspects of the grammar of the language are introduced and discussed as they come up in each dialogue. Again, it may be advisable to keep a notebook of these grammar items for revision later. Grammar is discussed in greater detail in Part II.

Since language reflects the culture of a people, aspects of the culture of the speakers of the language, such as the appropriate form of address for different categories of people, are highlighted and discussed as they come up in each dialogue. Lesson 17 deals with the language of specific cultural situations.

The most effective way to learn a new language is to practise speaking it as often as possible. It is hoped that anyone who is interested in learning to speak Twi will look out for Twi speakers and try to practise the language with them. In Ghana, most traders in the urban centres and taxi drivers speak Twi, and the learner who happens to be in the country is advised to try and communicate with them in Twi. The learner may discover that this is also a sure way of getting a good bargain!

I wish to take this opportunity to express my sincere thanks to Dr. Kofi K. Saah, Dr. Akosua Anyidoho and my daughter, Akuba, for their very valuable comments on an earlier version of this book.

Meda mo ase pii.

F.A.D.

December, 1995.

PART I

Getting Started with the Spoken Language

Lesson 1

THE TWI ALPHABET AND SOUNDS

The following are the letters of the Twi alphabet and the sounds associated with them.

a   a sound between the *a* in *a*pple and in c*a*lm
   eg. da: to sleep; daa: everyday.
   (Note: all Twi vowels can be either long or short.)
   When a occurs before i or u in a word, it has a different
   quality, represented in this book by [æ] as in
   daabi pronounced [dææbi] : no; Badu [bædu] : tenth born

b   eg. aba: seed

d   eg. di: to eat

e   stands for two sounds
   i. pronounced as the *a* in d*a*y.
      eg. dede: noise; seesei: now
   It often occurs in the same word with i or u
      eg. fie: house; bue: to open
   ii. pronounced as the *i* in s*i*t.
      eg. me: I; mee: to be full / to have eaten enough
   It often occurs in the same word with ɔ or ɛ
      eg. ɔhene: chief; adeɛ: thing

ɛ   pronounced as in g*e*t
   eg. ɛyɛ: it is good; fɛfɛɛfɛ: beautiful

f   eg. fa: to take

g   eg. gu: to scatter

h   eg. ɛhɔ: there

i   pronounced as in s*ea*t
   eg. di: to eat; pii: plenty

k   eg. kɔ: to go

l   eg. lɔre: lorry

m   eg. ma: to give

n   eg. nom: to drink

o   stands for two sounds
   i. pronounced as in g*o*
      eg. yoo: all right
   It often occurs with i or u in the same word.
      eg. owuo: death; bio: again
   ii. pronounced as in b*oo*k
      eg. bo: to be drunk; paanoo: bread

It often occurs with ɔ or ε in the same word.
    eg. akokɔ: chicken; εmo: rice

ɔ ρronounced as in *law*
    eg. tɔ: to buy; kɔkɔɔ: red
p eg. pam: to sew
r ᴗg. bra: to come
s eg. sũ: to cry
t eg. tɔ: to buy
u pronounced as in *do*
    eg. bu: to break; huuhuu: arrogant
w sᴛands for two sounds
    i. pronounced as in wall
      eg. wu: to die
    ii. pronounced yw and usually occurs before i, e, ε
      eg. awia: sun; we: to chew; wεn: to keep guard
y eg. yε / yɔ: to do

Digraphs (letter combinations)
dw pronounced jw, that is j with pursed/rounded lips
    eg. dwene: to think
gy pronounced j as in *judge*
    eg. gye: to receive
hw this is the same as the initial sound in the interjection,
    *wh*ew!
    eg. hwε: to look at
hy pronounced sh as in *sh*irt
    eg. hyε: to wear
kw pronounced like the initial consonant in *qu*ick
    eg. nkwan: soup
ky pronounced ch as in *ch*ur*ch*
    eg. εkyε: hat
nw pronounced nyw, that is ny with pursed/rounded lips
    eg. nwunu: to leak
ny pronounced as a combination of the two sounds. (It occurs
    in Spanish: ñ in España)
    eg. Onyame: God
tw pronounced chw, that is ch with pursed/rounded lips
    eg. Twi: the Twi language

Nasalized Vowels

Five vowels have a contrast between those that have a nasal quality and those that do not.

    eg. fi   to go out   fĩ   dirt

se	to sharpen	ɛsɛ̃	teeth
nsa	hand	nsã	drink / alcohol
to	to throw	tõ	to bake
hu	to blow air	hũ	to see

This difference is not represented in the Twi orthography. In this book nasality is marked on the vowel if it does not occur before or after m, n, ny or nw. Vowels that occur in this position are usually nasalized.

Tone

Akan is a tone language, which means that the pitch of the voice on which a word is pronounced can bring about a difference in the meanings of words that are otherwise identical, as in:

pàpá	(low-high)	father
pápá	(high-high)	good
pàpà	(low-low)	fan

A!má	(high-lower high/mid)	name of a girl
àmà	(low-low)	so that

(NOTE: The exclamation mark in A!má indicates that the following high tone is lower in pitch than the preceding one, hence the label: lower high / mid.)

Tone is not marked in Twi orthography, and this tradition is followed in this book. Experience has shown that tone marks on extended texts can be confusing, even for native speakers. Tone is best learnt by listening to the spoken language as said by an instructor or by listening to the tape that comes with this book over and over again. It is also useful for the learner to record his/her own spoken Twi, play it back, and compare it with the recording on the instructional tape. This helps in identifying what one is doing wrong.

Lesson 2

GREETINGS AND RESPONSES

A Everyday greetings

Mema wo akyĕ.	pronounced [maakyĕ]	Good morning.
(I-give you {sing.} morning)		
Mema wo ahǎ.	pronounced [maahǎ]	Good afternoon.
Mema wo adwo.	pronounced [maadwo]	Good evening.
Mema mo akyĕ / ahǎ / adwo.		Good morning /
(I-give you {plu.} morning etc.)		afternoon / evening.
Yɛma mo akyĕ / ahǎ / adwo.		Good morning /
(We-give you {plu.} morning etc.)		afternoon / evening.

Akwaaba.	Welcome.	
(you've gone and come back)		
Da yie.	Goodnight.	(response: Yoo.)
(sleep well)		
Nante yie.	Safe journey/	(response: Yoo.)
(walk well)	Goodbye.	

Responses

Yaa agya.	proper response to an older male (agya means father)
Yaa ɛna.	proper response to an older female (ɛna means mother)
Yaa ɔba.	proper response to a child by an adult (ɔba means child)
Yaa nua.	pronounced [yæænwĭǎ] proper response to a person your age (nua means brother / sister / cousin)
Yoo.	all right; a common response to 'nante yie' and 'da yie'

6

B Christmas and other festive occasions

(Mema wo) Afenhyia pa. (I wish {give} you) a good meeting of
                                            the year, i.e. the year has gone full cycle
(afe: year; nhyia: meeting; pa: good)

Note Christmas: buronya (from oburoni: 'whiteman'; nya: to
                            obtain / get; i.e. Oburoni has got something
                            to celebrate.)

Response
Afe nkɔ mmɛto yɛn bio.   May the year go (round) and come to
                            find us again.
(afe: year; nkɔ: may it go; mmɛ: may it come; to: catch up
with; yɛn: us; bio: again)

Dialogue 1

A: Awuraa, maakyĕ.   Good morning, ma'am/lady.
B: Yaa nua [yæænwĭǎ]   (response)
A: Wo hŏ te sɛn?   How are you?
   (your body is how)
B: Me hŏ yɛ.   I'm fine.
   (my body is good)
OR
A: Owura, maakyĕ.   Good morning, sir / gentleman.
B: Yaa nua [yæænwĭǎ].   (response)
A: ɛte sɛn?   How is it? (to someone your age
                                    or younger)
B: ɛyɛ.   Fine.
   (it is good)
OR
Child: Papa, maahǎ.   'Father', good afternoon.
Adult: Yaa ɔba.   (response)
       Wo hŏ te sɛn?   How are you?
Child: Mepa wo kyɛw,   Please,
       [mepaakyɛw] me hŏ yɛ.   I'm fine.

Christmas, New Year or any other festive occasion

A: Awuraa, afenhyia pa.   Happy meeting of the year,
                                    ma'am.
B: Afe nkɔ mmɛto yɛn bio.   May the year go and come to
                                    meet us again.

7

A: ɛte sɛn?   How is it?
B: (Onyame adom) ɛyɛ.   (By God's grace) fine.
                          (very formal adult response)

Culture points

1. People are usually expected to ask after each other's health. It is not enough to say 'Hello' or 'Hi'.
2. A child does not ask an adult 'how are you?' unless it is known that the adult is sick.
3. Children / younger people are expected to be polite when speaking to an adult.
4. It is usual for people to shake hands when they greet each other. 'Afenhyia pa' and 'akwaaba' are normally accompanied by a handshake, but everyday greetings may or may not be accompanied by a handshake. When it becomes necessary to shake hands with a number of people, this is done from right to left, that is, anti-clockwise.

Lesson 3

BEING POLITE

Mepa wo kyɛw. pronounced [mepaakyɛw]   Please/I beg you.
(I remove my hat to you)
Meda wo ase.   pronounced [medaase]   Thank you.
(I lay at your feet)

The following forms of address are used when one wants to be polite:

Owura	Sir / Mr
Brother	Older male, but not old enough to be your father.
Papa / Uncle	Father / uncle (for adult male old enough to be your father)
Wɔfa	Mother's brother / male cousin
Ɔpanyin	Elder (for elderly male)
Ɔbaa panyin	Female elder (for elderly female)
Awuraa	Lady / ma'am
Sister	Older female, but not old enough to be your mother
Maame/Auntie	Mother/Auntie (for adult female old enough to be your mother)
Sewaa	Father's sister / female cousin
Nana	Grandparent (also title for a male / female chief)

Dialogue 2

Amma :	Awuraa, maahǎ.	Good afternoon, (young) lady.
Abenaa :	Yaa ɛna.	(response)
Amma :	Wo maame wɔ hɔ?	Is your mother in?
Abenaa :	Auntie, mepa wo kyɛw [mepaakyɛw] ɔwɔ fie.	Please, Auntie, she's in the house.
Amma :	Frɛ no ma me, wae. (call her give me, 'please')	Call her for me, please.
Abenaa :	Mepaakyɛw merekɔfrɛ [meekɔfrɛ] no aba. (I'm-going-call her come)	Please, I'm going to call her.
Amma :	Yoo. Kɔ bra.	OK. Go and come.

9

Vocabulary

wɔ	to be	(ɛ)hɔ	there
fie	house / home	frɛ	to call
ma	to give / for		
ba (bra)	to come (the Imperative form is 'bra' : come!)		
wae	'please' (a term for coaxing a person to do something; also used when talking to a child; at times equivalent to 'OK'? The full form is 'woate?' : have you heard (me)?). It is used for a person your age or younger.		

EXERCISE

Say the following in Twi:
- Good morning, Ma'am / Sir.
- Good afternoon, 'father'/'mother'.
- Good evening, Ma'am /'mother'.
- Please, call Amma for me.
- I am going to call Amma.
- Your mother is at home.
- Is your father in?

Dialogue 3

Abenaa	: ɔpanyin, maakyɛ oo.	Good morning, elder.
Papa Kofi	: Yaa asɔn. Wo hõ te sɛn?	(response) How are you?
Abenaa	: Mepaakyɛw me hõ yɛ.	Please, I'm fine.
Papa Kofi	: Yɛda Onyame ase.	We thank God.
Abenaa	: ɔpanyin, mepaakyɛw Maame Yaa wɔ hɔ?	Elder, please, is Maame Yaa in?
Papa Kofi	: Aane, ɔwɔ fie.	Yes, she's at home.
	ɔwɔ gyaade.	She's in the kitchen.
Abenaa	: ɔpanyin, medaase.	Elder, thank you.

Vocabulary

asɔn	response to greeting, see culture points below
Onyame	God. Other names for God are: Otumfoɔ: The powerful one; Almighty (tumi : power) Twereduampɔn: The tree one leans against and does not fall. (twere: lean on; dua: tree; m-pɔn: not break off)
aane	yes
gyaade	kitchen

10

Culture points

1. Maakyɛ oo : Quite often 'oo' is added to the normal greeting as a sign of respect, especially if the person is some distance away from the speaker.
2. Yaa asɔn : There is a fixed number of responses to greetings in Akan, and every individual inherits his/her unique response from his/her father. Other such responses are : (Yaa) amu, aberaw, ahenewa, oburu, etc. It is considered impolite to use the wrong response for a person. In a small community, such as one finds in a village, people tend to know what response to use. However, 'asɔn' is generally considered neutral, and can be used for most people.
   For the learner, the responses in Lesson 2 are adequate.
3. 'Maame Yaa': one is always expected to show respect for older/senior people by addressing them with the correct title, such as:
   Nana / Maame / Sewaa / Auntie / Sister Amma
   Nana / Papa / Wɔfa / Uncle / Brother Kofi.

It is common to find young people who are called Maame/Nana Amma or Papa/Nana Kofi. This is because they were named after an older relation, and it is considered disrespectful to call them without the appropriate title.

Lesson 4

MAKING FRIENDS

Dialogue 4 : Getting to know somebody.

A:	Awuraa, maakyɛ̌.	Good morning, ma'am.
B:	Yaa nua [yæænwǐǎ].	(response)
A:	Mepaakyɛw yɛfrɛ wo sɛn?	Please, what is your name?
	(Please, what do they call you?)	
OR	Mepaakyɛw wo din de sɛn?	Please, what is your name?
	(Please, your name is what?)	
B:	Wɔfrɛ/Yɛfrɛ me Mary.	I'm called (they call me) Mary.
OR	Me din de Mary.	My name is called Mary.
OR	Mede Mary.	I'm called Mary.
A:	Me nso wɔfrɛ /yɛfrɛ me Kofi.	I also am called Kofi.
	Wɔwoo /Yɛwoo me Fiada.	I was born on a Friday.
Mary:	Kofi, wo hɔ̌ te sɛn?	Kofi, how are you?
	(Kofi, your body is how?)	
Kofi :	Me hɔ̌ yɛ.	I am well.
	Na wo nso ɛ?	And you too?
Mary:	Me nso me hɔ̌ yɛ.	I also am well.
Kofi :	Mary, worekɔ [wookɔ] hɛ̌?	Mary, where are you going?
Mary:	Merekɔ [meekɔ] Nkran.	I'm going to Accra.
Kofi :	Yoo, nante yie.	All right, goodbye (walk well).
	Yɛbɛhyia [yebehyia] bio.	We'll meet again / See you.
Mary:	Yoo.	OK.

Vocabulary

din	name
de	to bear / carry (a name)
sɛn?	how? / what?
te	to feel / hear / smell
yɛ	to be good / in a favourable state
hɔ̌	body / self
(ɛ)hɛ̌	where?
re-	Progressive prefix
bɛ-	Future prefix
hyia	to meet
bio	again

Grammar points

1. ɛ? is a question particle, as in

Wo nso ɛ?   You too?/ How about you?
Kofi ɛ?   How about Kofi?

2. *Pronouns*

Singular		Plural	
me	I	yɛn	we
wo	you	mo	you
ɔno	he/she/it	wɔn/wɔɔnom/	they
		ɔɔmo (also yɛn)	
ɛno	it (non-animate)		

Subject Pronouns

me-kɔ	I go	yɛ-kɔ	we go
wo-kɔ	you go	mo-kɔ	you go
ɔ-kɔ	s/he/it goes	wɔ-kɔ /	they go
ɛ-kɔ	it (eg. a car) goes	wɔɔnom kɔ/	
		yɛ-kɔ	they go

(most Asante speakers use yɛ- for both 'we' and 'they')

Object Pronouns

ɔfrɛ me. S/he calls me.	ɔfrɛ yɛn.	S/he calls us.
ɔfrɛ wo. S/he calls you.	ɔfrɛ mo.	S/he calls you.
ɔfrɛ no. S/he calls him/her.	ɔfrɛ wɔɔnom/ ɔɔmo.	S/he calls them.

Note: The 3rd person non-animate does not have an object pronoun, as illustrated by the following examples:

Fa   sika   no kɔ.   Fa kɔ.
Take money the go (take the money away).   Take go (take it away).

but   Fa abofra no kɔ.   Fa no kɔ.
Take the child away.   Take him/her away.

Other examples:

Metɔ paanoo.	I buy bread.	Metɔ.	I buy it.
ɔbɛfa mpa no.	S/he'll take the bed.	ɔbɛfa.	S/he'll take it.
Kɔgye sika no.	Go and take the money.	Kɔgye.	Go and take it.
ɔbɛtɔn kaa no.	S/he'll sell the car.	ɔbɛtɔn.	S/he'll sell it.

13

3. The Progressive form of the verb has the prefix 're' but this is not pronounced. It is realised as a long vowel, as shown below:

Merekɔ.	pronounced	[meekɔ]	I'm going.
Worekɔ.	pronounced	[wookɔ]	You're going.
ɔrekɔ.	pronounced	[ɔɔkɔ]	S/he / it is going.
ɛrekɔ.	pronounced	[ɛɛkɔ]	It (eg. a car) is going.

Culture points

The Akan people, that is including the Asante, give their children names according to the day of the week on which they were born, as shown below:

Days of the week		Boy's name	Girl's name
Sunday	Kwasiada	(A)Kwasi	Akosua
Monday	(ɛ)Dwoada	Kwadwo	Adwoa
Tuesday	(ɛ)Benada	Kwabena	Abenaa
Wednesday	Wukuada	Kwaku	Akua
Thursday	Yawoada	Yaw	Yaa
Friday	(E)Fiada	Kofi	Afua / Afia
Saturday	Memeneda	Kwame	Amma

See Appendix II for more information on Akan names.

EXERCISE

1. Look for an Almanac and find out your Akan day name and those of your friends and members of your family.
2. Say the following in Twi without looking at the dialogue:
   My name is ..... / They call me .....
   What is your name?
   How are you?
   I'm going to .....
   Good morning / afternoon, Ma'am / Sir / Kofi.
   See you.
   How is it?

Dialogue 5: Finding out where one comes from

Kofi :	Awuraa, maahå.	Good afternoon, ma'am.
Mary:	Yaa nua [yæænwlå].	(response)
Kofi :	Wo hõ te sɛn?	How are you?

14

Mary:	Me hổ yɛ.	I'm fine.
	Na wo nso ɛ?	And you too?
Kofi :	Me nso me hổ yɛ.	I also am well.
	Mepaakyɛw, wofi(ri) [wufi(ri)] hɛ̃?	Please, where are you from?
Mary:	Mefi [mifi] aburokyire.	I come from overseas.
	Mefi [mifi] Engiresi aburokyire.	I come from England (English overseas).
Kofi :	Wofi [wufi] kuro bɛn so?	Which town / city do you come from?
Mary:	Mefi [mifi] London.	I come from London.
Kofi :	London kuro kɛseɛ no?	London the big city?
Mary:	Aane. Adɛn, wonim [wunim] hɔ?	Yes. Why? Do you know the place?
Kofi :	Daabi [dæ æbi]. Mate din.	No. I've heard about it (the name).
	Na worekɔ [wookɔ] hɛ̃?	And where are you going?
Mary:	Merekɔ [meekɔ] Nkran.	I'm going to Accra.
Kofi :	ɛnneɛ, nante yie.	(Well) then, safe journey.
	(OR kɔ bra)	Goodbye (go and come).
	Yɛbɛhyia [yebehyia].	We'll meet (see you).
Mary:	Yoo.	OK.

Vocabulary

fi / firi	to come from
aburokyire	overseas (beyond the horizon; usually used to refer to Britain, Europe & America)
kuro	town
kɛseɛ	big
no	the (definite article)
adɛn?	why?
nim	to know
ɛnneɛ	then (conjunction) (from ɛno deɛ : in that case)

Grammar points

1. *Questions*
    Mary asks: 'Wonim hɔ?' Do you know the place?
The difference between this question and the following statement:
    'Wonim hɔ.' You know the place.
is in the intonation. The pitch of the voice falls at the end of the question, but it stays level at the end of the statement.

15

Here are more examples.

ɔkɔ. : He's gone.   Wonim no. : You know him.
ɔkɔ? : Has he gone?   Wonim no? : Do you know him?
Kɛseɛ no. : The big one.
Kɛseɛ no? : The big one?

Other questions are, of course, formed by using question words, as in:

     Wo hõ te *sɛn*?   How are you?
     Kuro *bɛn*?   Which town / city?
     Wo nso *ɛ*?   You also?

2. *Sentence structure*
   i. Like English, Twi sentences have the structure

Subject	Verb	Object
Wo	nim	hɔ.
You	know	there (the place).

Amma	fi	aburokyire.
Amma	comes from	overseas.

Identify similar sentence structures in the above dialogue.

   ii. Unlike English, however, adjectives (including the definite and indefinite articles) follow the nouns they qualify, as in:

Noun	Adjective
kuro	kɛseɛ
town / city	big
kuro	no
town / city	the

EXERCISE

Say the following in Twi:
    Please, where do you come from?
    I come from ....
    John /Amma comes from ....
    I know the big town.
    Do you know the big town?
    Which big town?
    Mary comes from overseas.
    She comes from England.

Dialogue 6   Finding out where one comes from

Kofi: Owura, maahå.	Good afternoon, sir.
John: Yaa nua [yæænwîå]	(response)
Kofi: Mepaakyɛw, yɛfrɛ wo sɛn?	Please, what is your name?
John: Yɛfrɛ me John.	My name is John.
Kofi: John, wo hõ te sɛn?	John, how are you?
John: Me hõ yɛ.	I'm fine.
Kofi: Mepaakyɛw, wofiri [wufiri] hɛ?	Please, (pardon my asking) where do you come from?
John: Mefi [mifi] America.	I come from America.
Kofi: Saa? Woyɛ Oburoni?	Really? Are you a 'whiteman'? (from beyond the seas?)
John: Aane. Meyɛ Obibini Buroni.	Yes, I'm an African 'oburoni'. (African-American / European)
Kofi: Wosɛ Ghanani paa.	You look very much like a Ghanaian.
Wobaa ha akyɛ anaa?	Have you been here long?
John: Aane, akyɛ kakra.	Yes, I've been here for some time (it's been a little long).
Kofi: Wote Twi paa.	You speak Twi very well.
Mo!	Congratulations!
Woayɛ [wayɛ] adeɛ.	You have done well.
John: Medaase.	Thank you.
Wo nso wofi(ri) [wufi(ri)] hɛ?	You too, where are you from?
Kofi: Mefi [mifi] Kumase.	I come from Kumasi.
Meyɛ Asanteni.	I'm an Asante.
John: ɛnneɛ mene wo bɛka Twi daa.	(Well) then, I'll speak Twi with you everyday.
Kofi: Yoo, mate.	OK. I have heard.

Vocabulary

Oburoni	someone from 'aburokyire' (normally translates as 'whiteman'/ European)
aburokyire	land beyond the horizon (from borɔ : horizon; akyire : back / behind)
Oburoni kɔkɔɔ	red 'Oburoni' (whiteman i.e. when one wants to be specific)
OR	
Oburoni fitaa	white 'Oburoni'
Obibini	African (any black person)
Abibiman/ (Abibirem)	Africa (biri : to be black; man : country)

17

saa?	really?
sɛ	to look like / resemble
(ɛ)ha	here
kyɛ(re)	to stay long / delay
kakra	a little
paa	very
mo!	congratulations! / well done!
yɛ adeɛ	to do something admirable
	(yɛ: to do; adeɛ: thing)

Grammar points

1. 'ni' from 'oni' (person) is added to place names to indicate that one is a citizen of that place.

Oburoni :	someone from Aburokyire
Asanteni :	someone from the Asante area of Ghana
Nkrani / Ɔkrani:	someone from Accra (Nkran), a Gã
Germanni:	a German
Nigeriani :	a Nigerian
Zimbabweni :	a Zimbabwean
Obibini :	an African, from Abibirem, the land of black people

EXERCISE

Say the following in Twi:
I am a Californian.
Mary is an African-American.
John is a New Yorker.
Kofi is an Asante.
Esi is a Fante.
Alice is a Londoner.

2. In the dialogue, there are instances where subject pronouns have two different pronunciations associated with them:

me-yɛ	me-fi [mi-fi]
I am	I come from

wo-sɛ	wo-fi(ri) [wu-firi]
you-look like	you-come from

Twi verbal prefixes, including subject pronouns, have two pronunciations depending on the vowel of the verb stem, so that the nine vowels of the language fall into two groups. In general, only vowels of one group will occur in

18

any given word. This is a very common feature of the language, and is referred to as vowel harmony.

Group 1		Group 2	
e ɛ ɔ o a		i e o u	
meba	I come	mefi [mifi]	I come from
woba	you come	wofi(ri) [wufiri]	you come from
ɔrekɔ	s/he/it is going	ɔrebu	s/he/it is breaking
[ɔɔkɔ]		[oobu]	it
yɛbɛte	we will hear	yɛbɛhyia [yebehyia]	we will meet
ɔsɛ	s/he looks like	ɔhũ [ohũ]	s/he/it sees
ɛkɔ	it (eg. a car) goes	ɛbu [ebu]	it breaks
moba	you (plu) come	mohũ [muhũ]	you (plu) see

The two diferent pronunciations for the verbal prefixes above are illustrated below. The verbs used are 'kɔ' : to go; 'bu' : to break.

Pronouns	Group 1	Group 2
1st pers. sing.	me- kɔ	mi- bu
2nd pers. sing.	wo- kɔ	wu- bu
3rd pers. sing. (animate)	ɔ- kɔ	o- bu
3rd pers. sing. (non-animate)	ɛ- kɔ	e- bu
1st pers. plu.	yɛ- kɔ	ye- bu
2nd pers. plu.	mo- kɔ	mu- bu
3rd pers. plu.	wɔɔnom (not a prefix, no change)	
	wɔ- kɔ	wo- bu
	yɛ- kɔ	ye- bu
Progressive: same as pronoun prefixes, but long vowel		
eg.	mee- kɔ	mii- bu
	woo-kɔ	wuu- bu
	ɔɔ- kɔ	oo- bu
Future:	bɛ- kɔ	be- bu

Note : There are two pronunciations associated with each of the vowel letters e and o.
i) For Group 1 prefixes e is pronounced as in 'si*t*' and o as in 'b*oo*k'.
ii) For Group 2 prefixes e is pronounced as in 'd*a*y' and o as in 'g*o*'.

EXERCISE

1. Practise the pronunciation of the following verbs, as well as those above.

ɔfrɛ	s/he calls	ɔfiri [ofiri]	s/he comes from
yɛkɔ	we go	yɛhũ [yehũ]	we see it
ɔbɛte	s/he'll hear it	ɔbɛdi [obedi]	s/he'll eat it
mofa	you take it	motie [mutie]	you listen

The verb stems in these examples are:

Group 1
frɛ	to call
kɔ	to go
te	to hear
fa	to take

Group 2
firi	to come from
hũ	to see / consult
di	to eat
tie	to listen

2. Use the appropriate verbal prefixes to make up the Habitual, Progressive and the Future forms for each verb.

Lesson 5

FINDING OUT WHAT ONE DOES

Dialogue 7

Amma: Mary, maakyĕ.	Good morning, Mary.
Mary: Yaa nua.	(response)
Amma, ɛte sɛn?	Amma, how is it?
Amma: ɛyɛ, na wo nso ɛ?	Fine, and you?
Mary: Me nso me hŏ yɛ.	I also am fine.
Amma: Mary, woreyɛ [wooyɛ] deɛn wɔ Ghana?	Mary, what are you doing in Ghana?
	(you are doing what in Ghana?)
Mary: Meyɛ osûǎni [oswǐæni] wɔ ha. Mewɔ Legon, sûǎpɔn no mu.	I'm a student here. I'm in the University (the great institution) at Legon.
Amma: Saa?	Is that so?
Me nso meyɛ osûǎni wɔ Legon.	I also am a student at Legon.
Wobaa Legon akyɛ anaa?	Have you been in Legon long?
Mary: Madi [mædi] bosome baakŏ ne naawɔtwe mmienu.	I've been (spent) here one month and two weeks.
Amma: Wobɛkyɛ?	Will you stay long?
Mary: Mɛdi [medi] mfeɛ mmienu ne abosome nsǐǎ.	I will be here for (spend) two years and six months.
Mepɛ sɛ mesûǎ [miswǐǎ] Twi kasa yie paa.	I want to learn the Twi language very well indeed.
Amma: ɛnneɛ mɛfa wo adamfo.	In that case, I will be your (will take you as my) friend.
Me ne wo bɛkǎ Twi daa.	I and you will speak Twi every day.
Mary: Medaase pii.	Thank you very much.
Amma: Merekɔ laibri.	I'm going to the library.
Yɛbɛhyia [yebehyia] bio.	We'll meet again / see you.
Mary: Yoo.	OK.

Vocabulary

(ɛ)deɛn / dɛn?	what?
osûǎni	student (from sûǎ : to learn; oni : person)
wɔ	at / in (locative verb)

21

sûápɔn	University (sûá: to learn; pɔn: great/important)
kyɛ(re)	delay / keep long
di	to eat; often used with other words to express various things.
	eg. di afe : to spend a year
	di asɛm : to settle a case / to judge
anaa?	question word; optional after questions requiring the answer 'yes' or 'no'.
	eg. ɔkɔ (anaa?): has he gone?
abosome	months
bosome	month
naawɔtwe	week (from nna : days; nnwɔtwe : eight)
mfeɛ	years
afe	year
mmienu	two (see numbers below)
pɛ	to like / want
sɛ	that (conjunction)
kasa	language
adamfo	friend
nnamfo	friends
kã	to say / speak
daa	everyday (from da: day)

Numbers

1	baakõ	11	du baakõ	21	aduonu baakõ
2	mmienu	12	du mmienu	22	aduonu mmiennu
3	mmeɛnsã	13	du mmeɛnsã	23	aduonu mmeɛnsã
4	(ɛ)nan	14	du nan	24	aduonu nan
5	(e)num	15	du num	25	aduonu num
6	(e)nsĩã	16	du nsĩã	26	aduonu nsĩã
7	(ɛ)nson	17	du nson	27	aduonu nson
8	nwɔtwe	18	du nwɔtwe	28	aduonu nwɔtwe
9	(ɛ)nkron	19	du nkron	29	aduonu nkron
10	(e)du	20	aduonu	30	aduasã

EXERCISE

1. Give the Twi numbers for 31 to 39.
2. 40 is 'aduanan', what is 42?
3. Exercise on vowel harmony:
   The following verbs occur in the dialogue, showing how verbal prefixes are affected by vowel harmony.

mepɛ	I want	mesûã [miswĩã]	I learn
wobɛkyɛ	you'll stay long	yɛbɛhyia [yebehyia]	we'll meet

22

Use the appropriate vowel in the verbal prefix to complete the following sentences:

Group 1	Group 2
__te Twi.	__di paanoo.
S/he understands Twi.	S/he eats bread.
__sɛ me papa.	__nim no.
I look like my father.	I know him/her.
__sɛ wo maame.	__nim Kofi.
You look like your mother.	You know Kofi.
__ __kɔ hɔ.	__ __hû no.
S/he will go there.	S/he will see him/her.
__ __ kae.	__ __ tie.
You will remember.	You will listen
__ kɔ	__ suro.
I fight.	I'm afraid.

Note: Only i and u, among the Group 2 vowels, occur as the first vowel in verb stems in Asante Twi. Verbs with i and u vowels have Group 2 vowels in the prefixes. Other verbs have Group 1 vowels in the prefixes.

Grammar points

1. Plural nouns : nouns form their plurals by either
   i. adding a prefix a- especially where the singular noun has a prefix e-, ɛ-, o- or ɔ-. They may also have a suffix '-foɔ', especially if the singular has the suffix '-ni'.

   eg. edu (10) : aduonu 20;   osûáni : asûáfoɔ   students
        ɔdan :   adan   houses;   bosome : abosome   months

OR

   ii. adding a prefix m- before p b f m; or n- before other consonants especially where the singular noun begins with the prefix a-.
   eg. afe :   mfeɛ   years;   da :   nna   days
      (ɛ)toa : ntoa   bottles;   adamfo : nnamfo   friends

Note: Where the plural marker m- or n- occurs before b, d, g, gy or dw these are pronounced as long mm or nn.

   eg. odwan : nnwan   sheep;   abofra : mmofra   children

This change in the consonant is also true of negative forms of verbs.

23

eg. di : eat it	nni : don't eat it
ɔba : s/he comes	ɔmma : s/he doesn't come

2. As noted earlier (Dialogue 5), adjectives occur after the nouns they qualify.

eg. afe baakõ : one year;   mfeε mmienu : two years

3. The Perfect form of the verb

    This is indicated by the prefix a-. In the first person singular, the vowel of the pronoun prefix me- is dropped before the Perfect prefix, hence madi (from me + adi) : I have eaten.

    In the third person singular, the pronoun prefix ɔ- and the Perfect prefix a- are pronounced [wa-], as in ɔafa [wafa] : s/he has taken it.

EXERCISE

Complete the following sentences by filling in the blank spaces with the appropriate words.

Kofi _____ _____ nsiã.
Kofi is six years old.

Me maame _____ _____ _____ mmienu.
My mother is forty two years old.

_____ ntoa ____ nwɔtwe.
S/he has taken eighteen bottles.

Mewɔ _____ _____
I have three friends.

Amma bɛtɔ _____ _____
Amma will buy two sheep.

Auntie Abenaa wɔ _____ _____
Auntie Abenaa has four houses.

Madi _____ _____ wɔ ha.
I have spent nine months here.

Lesson 6

FINDING OUT WHERE ONE LIVES

Dialogue 8

Kofi: John, maahã.	Good afternoon, John.
John: Yaa nua.	(response)
Kofi: ɛte sɛn?	How is it?
John: ɛyɛ; na wo nso ɛ?	Fine; and you?
Kofi: Me nso me hõ yɛ.	I am also well.
John, wote hɛ̃?	John, where do you live?
John: Mewɔ Akuafo Hall.	I'm in Akuafo Hall.
Medan nɔma yɛ aduasã nsĩã wɔ K Block.	My room number is 36 in K Block.
Kofi: Me deɛ mete me papa fie.	As for me I live in my father's house.
Yɛn nɔma yɛ (yɛn dan tɔ so) aduonu mmeɛnsa wɔ West Legon.	Our number is 23 (our house is the 23rd in) West Legon.
Akyire yi mɛba abɛsra wo.	Later, I'll come and visit you.
Mpo ɔkyena mɛba abɛsra wo.	Actually (even) tomorrow I'll come and visit you.
John: Yoo, mɛhwɛ w'anim [wænim]	All right, I'll expect you (I'll look out for your face).

Vocabulary

te	to live in a place / to sit
deɛ	emphatic particle
akyire yi	later (akyire : the back of / behind; yi : this)
mpo	even / in fact
ɔkyena	tomorrow

other expressions of time :

anɔpa	morning	(ɛ)nnora	yesterday
awia	afternoon (sun)	ɛnnɛ	today
anwumerɛ	evening	ɔkyena	tomorrow
anadwo	night		

sra	to visit
hwɛ	look / look at
anim	face (from ani : eye; mu: inside)
w'anim	your face (contracted form for 'wo anim')

25

Grammar points

1. Emphatic particle: the subject pronoun is repeated after the emphatic particle

   eg. Kofi deɛ ɔte Twi.   As for Kofi he speaks Twi.

   John na ɔnte Twi.   It is John who does not speak Twi.

2. hwɛ anim : to expect (to look at / look out for one's face)
   There are a number of idiomatic expressions with body part words:

   eg. ani gye : to be happy (the eyes have received)

   ani wu : to be ashamed (eyes are dead)

   eg. N'ani awu. : S/he is ashamed.

   asõ yɛ den : to be stubborn (the ears are hard)

   eg. W'asõ yɛ den. : You are stubborn.

   See Appendix I for more examples.

3. w'anim : your face (contracted form for wo anim)

   Possessive Pronouns

1st pers. sing.	me	1st pers. plu.	yɛn
2nd pers. sing.	wo	2nd pers. plu.	mo
3rd pers. sing.	ne	3rd pers. plu.	wɔɔnom/ ɔɔmo

   When a singular possessive pronoun occurs before a noun that begins with a vowel, the vowel of the pronoun is dropped, resulting in a contracted form. Plural possessive pronouns (except the 1st person plural) do not use a contracted form. The following examples illustrate these points.

m'ataadeɛ	my dress	y'ataadeɛ	our dress
w'ani	your eye(s)	mo ani	your eyes
n'adamfo	his/her friend	wɔɔnom adamfo	their friend

   Before nouns that begin with a consonant, there is no change, as in:

me dan	my house	yɛn dan	our house
wo ti	your head	mo ti	your heads
ne ntoma	his/her cloth	wɔɔnom ntoma	their cloth

4. As stated in Lesson 1, there are two pronunciations associated with the vowel letter 'a'. The second one is represented as [æ] in this book. It is a Group 2 vowel, but

it does not occur by itself like the other vowels. It normally
occurs before the vowels i and u, as in the following
examples.

Group 1		Group 2	
daakyɛ̌	some day	daabi [dææbi]	no
ano	mouth	ani [æni]	eye(s)
adeɛ	thing	aduro [æduro]	medicine/drug
abɛ	oil palm	Badu [bædu]	tenth born

EXERCISE

Make up five sentences each with the emphatic particles 'deɛ'
and 'na'.

Examples:

Me deɛ mefi [mifi] Kumase.   As for me I come from Kumasi.
Amma na ɔfi [ofi] Nkran.   It is Amma who comes from
Accra.

Lesson 7

FINDING OUT EACH OTHER'S INTERESTS

Dialogue 9

Amma:	Mary, maadwo.	Good evening, Mary.
Mary:	Yaa nua.	(response)
Amma:	Wo mpɔ mu [mpom] te sɛn?	How are you (your joints)?
	OR	
	Mpɔ mu [mpom] ɛ?	
Mary:	Me hŏ yɛ, na wo nso ɛ?	I'm fine, and you?
Amma:	Me nso me hŏ yɛ.	I also am well.
	Mary, worekɔ hě?	Mary, where are you going?
Mary:	Merekɔ disko bi wɔ Osu.	I'm going to a disco in Osu (a suburb of Accra).
Amma:	Me nso merekɔ Nkran.	I also am going to Accra.
	Merekɔhwɛ sini.	I'm going to see a film/movie (cinema).
Mary:	Sini bɛn?	Which film / movie?
Amma:	ɛyɛ Michael Jackson sini.	It is a Michael Jackson film.
	M'ani [mæni] gye ne hŏ paa.	I like him very much. (I'm very happy about him).
Mary:	Saa? Me nso m'ani [mæni] gye ne hŏ paa.	Is that so? I also like him very much.
	Mede ne nnwom pii fi America bae.	I came with many of his songs from America. (I took many of his songs from America and came.)
Amma:	ɛwɔ kasɛt so anaa?	Are they on cassette?
Mary:	Aane.	Yes.
Amma:	ɛnneɛ mɛba abɛgye abɔ bi.	Then I'll come for (receive) them and play (some).
Mary:	Yoo. Mɛhwɛ w'anim.	All right. I'll expect you.
Amma:	Yoo. Baae.	All right. Goodbye.

Vocabulary

mpɔ mu	how are you (inside the joints)? (this is an alternative to 'Wo ho te sɛn?'/ 'ɛte sɛn?')
ɛpɔ	knot

28

(e)mu	inside
bi	indefinite article: a / a certain / some
ani gye ne hõ	to like (be happy about) somebody
de	to take (usually used with other verbs)
de ... ba	take ... come (i.e. bring)
de ... ma	take ... gïve (i.e. give to)
nnwom	song(s)
pii	plenty / many
gye	receive
bɔ	to play (eg music or a game)

Grammar points

1. Serial verbs

    Mary :   Mede ne nnwom pii fi America bae.
          (I-take his songs many from America came)
    Amma : Mɛba abɛgye abɔ.
          (I'll-come will-receive {and} play)

It is common to have a series of verbs (serial verbs) like these in a sentence. As pointed out under vocabulary, 'de' (to take) is usually used with other verbs in such constructions.
Other examples:

ɔde   kyɛ no bɛhyɛ.   S/he will wear the hat.
(s/he-take hat the will-wear)
Mede   nsuo no rekɔ hɔ.   I'm taking the water there.
(I-take water the going there)
ɔde   abofra no ba ha.   S/he brings the child here.
(s/he-take child the come here)

Note that the verb 'de' stays the same. It is the subsequent verb that indicates the tense, as in the first two examples above.

2. The Past form of the verb
This is indicated by the suffix -e if it is a verb with Group 1 vowels, and by -i if it is a verb with Group 2 vowels, as in the examples below:

Mebae.	I came.	Mehui [mihui]	I saw it.
ɔkɔe.	He went.	ɔdii [odii]	He ate it.
Yɛhwɛe.	We looked at it.	Yɛtui [yetui]	We dug it up.

When there is a complement after the verb, the suffix is realised as a lengthening of the final vowel or consonant of

29

the verb, as in the following examples:

Mebaa ha. I came here. Mehuu [mihuu] no. I saw him/her.
ɔkɔɔ hɔ. S/he went there. ɔdii [odii] ɛmo. S/he ate rice.
Yɛhwɛɛ wo. Yɛtuu [yetuu] bayerɛ.
We looked at you. We dug up yam.
ɔnomm nsuo. ɔdumm [odumm] gya no.
S/he drank water. S/he put out the fire.

EXERCISE

1. Serial verbs : Say the following sentences in Twi, using the
    verbs at the end of each sentence.
    I'm taking you home (fie). de.....kɔ
    Amma will bring the car here. de.....ba
    Amma wears the dress (ataadeɛ). de.....hyɛ
    S/he will bring me the hat (ɛkyɛ). de.....ma
    Note: The Future prefix is 'bɛ-'.

2. Past forms of the verb : express the following sentences in
    Twi.
    I went. I went home.
    You (plu.) bought it. You (plu.) bought a car.
    Kofi saw it. Kofi saw me.
    I sold it. I sold a hat. (sell: tɔn)

3. Choose the correct form of the verb to complete the following
    sentences:

    I took money. Mefae / mefaa / merefa sika.
    Kofi will see him/her. Kofi rehu / huu / bɛhu no.
    Afua goes home everyday. Afua bɛkɔ / kɔ / kɔɔ fie daa.
    Yaa sold bananas. Yaa retɔn / tɔnn / tɔnee kwadu.
    S/he will go home. ɔrekɔ / ɔkɔɔ / ɔbɛkɔ fie.
    Kofi is singing. Kofi bɛto / too / reto nnwom.

Dialogue 10

Kofi: John, maahã. Good afternoon, John.
John: Yaa nua. (response)
      ɛte sɛn? How is it?
Kofi: ɛyɛ. Na wo nso ɛ? Fine, and you?
John: ɛyɛ. Worekɔ hɛ̃? Fine. Where are you going?

30

Kofi:	Merekɔ steedium.	I'm going to the stadium.
	Merekɔhwɛ futbɔɔl.	I'm going to watch football.
	Agorɔ a Amɛrikafoɔ frɛ	The game which Americans call
	no sɔka no.	soccer.
	Kɔtɔkɔ ne Black Stars na	It is Kotoko and the Black Stars
	ɛrebɔ [ɛɛbɔ].	who are playing.
John:	Sɔka deɛ m'ani nnye hɔ̃.	As for soccer I'm not fond of it.
	Baskɛt bɔɔl na mepɛ.	It is basket ball that I like.
Kofi:	Ampa, mo Amɛrikafoɔ deɛ	True, you Americans
	mompɛ sɔka papa.	don't like soccer much.
	Ghana deɛ sɔka yɛ agorɔ	In Ghana soccer is a big/ very
	kɛseɛ.	popular game.
	ɛmmaa ne mmarima	Both (all) women and men
	[mmɛɛma] nyinaa hwɛ.	watch it.
John:	Twɛn me.	Wait for me.
	Mereba seesei ara.	I'm coming right now.
	Me ne wo bɛkɔ akɔhwɛ.	I and you will go and watch it.
Kofi:	Yoo, meretwɛn wo.	OK. I'm waiting for you.

Vocabulary

agorɔ	game / any playful activity
di agorɔ	to play
pɛ agorɔ	to be playful / friendly
ampa	true (for affirmation only; not used as an adjective) 'nokorɛ' is the adjective, as in asɛm nokorɛ: true story)
ani nnye hɔ̃	not fond of / not happy about
pɛ	to like / to want
(ɛ)mmaa	women (ɔbaa : woman / female)
mmarima	men (ɔbarima : man / male)
nyinaa	all/ both, when only two things are referred to
twɛn	to wait
seesei	now
seesei (ara)	(right) now

Grammar points

Negative form of the verb: As explained in Lesson 4 the negative form of the verb is indicated by a prefix m or n before the verb stem, as in

Mepɛ Baskɛt bɔɔl.	I like Basket ball.
Mempɛ sɔka.	I don't like soccer.

31

ɔtɔn kwadu.	S/he sells bananas.
ɔntɔn kwadu.	S/he doesn't sell bananas.
M'ani gye hɔ.	I like it.
M'ani nnye hɔ.	I don't like it.

Like the plural nouns which have a prefix m- or n-, when the negative prefix occurs before b, d, gy or dw the two sounds are pronounced mm, nn, nny, and nnw respectively, as in:

ɔba ha.	S/he comes here.
ɔmma ha.	S/he doesn't come here.
Medi [midi].	I eat it.
Menni [minni].	I don't eat it.
Gye.	Take / receive it.
Nnye.	Don't take it.
Dwene hɔ.	Think about it.
Nnwene hɔ.	Don't think about it.

EXERCISE

Say the negative of the following sentences; make up others of your own.

Mepɛ aborɔbɛ.	I like pineapple(s).
ɔkɔ sukuu.	S/he goes to school.
Mehwɛ sini.	I watch films / movies.
Kofi di ankaa.	Kofi eats oranges.
Amma bɔ nnwom.	Amma plays songs.
ɛyɛ me tikya.	It is my teacher.

Lesson 8

BUYING AND BARGAINING

Useful expressions

1.	Wei yɛ sɛn?	How much is this?
2.	Wei sɛn?	This, how much?
3.	Mepaakyɛw ɛyɛ sɛn?	Please, how much is it?
4.	ɛyɛ sidi apem (anaa)?	Is it a thousand cedis?
5.	Wose ɛyɛ sidi mpem du?	Do you say it is C10,000?
6.	Mepaakyɛw te so.	Please, reduce it (the price).
7.	Wonte so?	Won't you reduce it?
8.	Mɛtua [metua] sidi mpem nson.	I'll pay seven thousand cedis.
9.	Ne boɔ yɛ den.	It is expensive. (the price is hard / stiff)
10.	Ne boɔ yɛ den dodo.	It is too expensive.
11.	ɛyɛ fɛ paa.	It is very beautiful.
12.	Wei nyɛ fɛ koraa.	This one is not nice at all.
13.	Mɛtɔ mmienu.	I'll buy two of them.
14.	Ankaa wura.	Orange seller (owner of oranges).
15.	Ankaa no (yɛ) sɛn?	How much (are) the oranges?
16.	Mmeɛnsa yɛ sidi ɔha?	Are they three for a hundred cedis?
17.	ɛyɛ dɛ?	Is it (are they) sweet?
18.	Abere?	Is it (are they) ripe?
19.	Mɛtɔ (ankaa) sidi ahaasã.	I'll buy C300 worth (of oranges).
20.	Kwadu [kwædu] wura.	Banana seller.
21.	Mɛtɔ sidi ahaanu.	I'll buy C200 worth.
22.	To so.	Add a 'dash' (a few more as a gift).
23.	Ntosoɔ wɔ hɛ̃?	Where is (the) 'dash'?
24.	Ntosoɔ no sua [swa].	The dash is small.
25.	ɛsua [eswa].	It is small.
26.	Wotɔn nkateɛ?	Do you sell groundnuts (peanuts)?
27.	Nkateɛ no asã anaa?	Are the groundnuts finished?
28.	Ma me sidi ɔha.	Give me a C100 worth.

Vocabulary

wei	this	sɛn?	how much?
apem	thousand	te so	reduce the price
mpem	(plural)		(take off the top)

33

tua	to pay	(ε)boɔ	price
dodo	too much	tɔ	to buy
koraa	at all; used only in negative sentences		

eg. ɛyɛ paa : it is very good
ɛnyɛ koraa : it isn't good at all
mewɔ bi : I have some
menni bi koraa : I don't have any at all

ankaa	orange(s)
(o)wura	master / owner
dɛ	sweet
bere	to be ripe (some oranges are green in colour even when ripe)
kwadu [kwædu]	banana(s)

to so	add some as gift	sua [swa]	to be small
ntosoɔ	(noun)	tɔn	to sell
nkateɛ	groundnuts/peanuts		
sã	to be finished		
ɔha	100	ahaanu	200
ahaasã	300	ahanan	400

What do you think is the Twi for 500, 600, 700, 800, 900?

Grammar points

1. to so (verb)   ntosoɔ (noun)
   One way of making nouns from verbs is by adding a prefix
   m- or n- to the verb. There may or may not be a suffix as
   well.

eg. hyia	to meet	nhyiamu	meeting
sisi	to cheat	nsisie	cheating
bara	to forbid	mmara	law(s)/regulations
te aseɛ	to understand	nteaseɛ	understanding
sesã	to give change	nsesã	change

2. The prefix for the Future form of the verb is bɛ-, as in

ɔbɛba.	S/he will come.
Yɛbɛhyia [yebehyia].	We'll meet. / See you.

   When this prefix occurs with the first person singular
   subject pronoun, the pronoun 'me' and the Future prefix
   'bɛ' become 'mɛ' as in

Mɛtɔ.	I'll buy it.	Mɛtua [metua].	I'll pay.
Mɛgye.	I'll receive it.	Mɛdi [medi].	I'll eat it.
Mɛfa.	I'll take it.	Mɛhũ [mehũ].	I'll see it.

Culture points

1. Goods sold in the markets and along the sides of the street do not usually have fixed prices. One is therefore expected to bargain with the seller. However, the prices of goods in the shops are fixed, so one does not normally bargain in shops. Occasionally, especially if it is a small shop, a customer may ask for a discount or a reduction in price.

    (It is also normal to bargain with a taxi driver if you are going to a place outside the normal route that he uses. See Lesson 8 below.)
2. Fruit and vegetable sellers usually add a few of the items they are selling as gift, especially if the customer buys a sizeable quantity. This is 'ntosoɔ' loosely translated here as 'dash'.
3. It is considered rude to give or receive anything with the left hand. The right hand must always be used. If for some reason this is not possible, and the left hand must be used, the person says *Memma wo abenkum* (I don't give you my left (hand)), that is, 'Pardon my use of my left hand.'

EXERCISE

1. You want to buy oranges / bananas / groundnuts / pineapple (aborɔbɛ). Make up a dialogue between you and the seller, using the expressions you have learnt in this lesson.
2. Make up five sentences each with
    i) paa (very much)
    ii) koraa (at all)
   to indicate the things you like (pɛ) and the things you don't like.

Dialogue 11

Seller:	Kɔkɔɔkɔ.	Knocking.
Buyer:	Bra mu	Come in.
Seller:	Papa / Agya maadwo oo.	Good evening, 'father'.
Buyer:	Yaa ɔba.	(response for a child / much younger person)
Seller:	Papa mepaakyɛw metɔn ntaadeɛ.	Please, 'father', I sell clothes. (dresses).
Buyer:	Saa? ɛyɛ fɛ?	Is that so? Are they nice/ beautiful?

35

Seller: Mepaakyɛw, aane.	Please, yes.
Buyer: Ma menhwɛ.	Let me see it/have a look.
Metɔ a wobɛte so?	If I buy (it) will you reduce (the price)?
Seller: Papa mepaakyɛw yɛnte so.	Please, father, we don't reduce it (the price).
Buyer: Adɛn? ɛyɛ sotɔɔ mu adee?	Why? Is it (a thing) in a store (shop)?
Mepɛ sɛ metɔ bi ma me ba.	I want to buy one/some for my child.
Seller: Saa? Kɔkɔɔ yi yɛ fɛ.	Is that so? This red one is nice
ɛbɛfata wo ba no.	It will be nice on your child.
ɛyɛ sidi mpem nsĩã pɛ.	It is only C6,000.
Buyer: Ma menhwɛ.	Let me see it.
ɛyɛ fɛ ampa.	It is nice, true. (It is really nice.)
Seller: Papa, tɔ ma no.	Papa, buy it for her.
ɛbɛfata wo ba no paa.	It will really be nice on your child.
Buyer: Na fitaa yi ɛ?	How about this white one? (And this white one?)
Seller: ɛno nyɛ fɛ papa.	That one is not very nice.
Fa kɔkɔɔ no.	Take the red one.
ɛno na ɛbɛfata wo ba no paa.	It is that which will really be nice on your child.
Buyer: Yoo, mate.	OK. I've heard (you).
Wose ɛyɛ sidi mpem nsĩã?	You say it is C6,000?
Te so ɛ?	Won't you reduce it? (Reduce it?)
Seller: Mɛyi [meyi] so sidi ahanum.	I'll take off C500.
Fa no sidi mpem num ahanum [ahænum].	Take it for five thousand five hundred cedis.
Buyer: Yoo, merekɔfa sika aba.	OK. I'm going to bring (take money come) money.
ɛno ni(e).	Here it is.
Seller: Medaase pii.	Thank you very much.
Buyer: Aseda nni mu / Yɛnni [yenni] aseda	No need for thanks / We don't owe (each other) thanks.
Seller: Papa mepaakyɛw, merekɔ.	Please Papa, I'm going / leaving.
Buyer: Yoo, ɛkwan da hɔ.	OK. you may go (the road is clear).

36

Vocabulary

kɔkɔɔkɔ	knocking	ɔba	child
sotɔɔ	store / shop	mma	children
adeɛ	thing	ataadeɛ	dress
fɛ	beautiful	ntaadeɛ	dresses
sɛ	that (conjunction)		
fata	to look nice on a person (of clothes)		
kɔkɔɔ	red		
fitaa	white		
se	to say		
nni	not have (always used to negate 'wɔ' : mewɔ bi : I have some; menni bi : I don't have any ɛwɔ ha : It is here ; ɛnni ha : It is not here.)		
aseda	thanks (noun, from da ase : to thank)		
ɛkwan da hɔ	permission granted (the way is clear)		
ɛkwan	road / way		

Colour adjectives: The most common / frequently used colour
adjectives are kɔkɔɔ : red;   fitaa : white;
tuntum : black or any very dark colour.
Others, less common, are: ahabammono: green, the colour
of fresh (mono) leaf (ahaban);
akokɔsradeɛ : yellow, the colour of the fat (sradeɛ) of
chicken (akokɔ).

EXERCISE

1. Use the colour words to describe your clothes; your shoes
(mpaboa) and things in your room.
2. Use 'wɔ' (have) and 'nni' (not have) to make up sentences
indicating some of the things you have and those you do not
have.

Culture points

1. Africans show a lot of respect for age and seniority. In the
dialogue the younger person addresses the older person as
'Papa' (father) even though the man is not his/her father. The
seller also starts much of what s/he says with 'Please'.
2. There are two expressions for announcing one's presence on
entering a house:
    a)   kɔkɔɔkɔ : knocking (mimicking the sound made when
    knocking on a door)

bra mu : come in (response to 'kɔkɔɔkɔ')

b) agoo : knocking (also used for getting attention when one wants to speak at a gathering, or when one wants to push one's way through a crowd)

amee : (response to 'agoo'; no special meaning)

Lesson 9

TRAVELLING WITHIN TOWN

Useful expressions

1. Draeva wereko he? — Driver where are you going?
2. Wereko Nkran? — Are you going to Accra?
3. Mereko Osu. — I'm going to Osu.
4. Wobegye sen? — What is the fare? (How much will you take?)
5. Wobegye sidi apem? — You will charge C1,000?
6. Saa na yegye anaa? — Is that the normal fare? (Is that what they take?)
7. Yennye saa. — That is not the fare. (They don't take that.)
8. Te so. — Reduce it.
9. Menni sika. — I don't have money.
10. Me sika sua [swa]. — My money is small.
    Enso. — It won't be enough.
11. Mema wo sidi ahanson. — I will give you C700.
12. Wonnye saa? — You won't take that?
13. Mema wo sidi ahanwotwe. — I'll give you C800.
14. Mesi [mesi] wo edan kesee no anim. — I will get down in front of the big house.
15. Mesi ha. — I'll get down here.
16. Mepaakyew gyina ha. — Please stop here.
17. Gyina edan kesee no anim. — Stop in front of the big house.
18. Sika no ni. — Here's the money.
19. Eye sidi apem. — It is C1,000.
20. Me nsesa ye sidi ahaanu. — My change is C200.

Vocabulary

sua [swa]	to be small
so	to be enough / adequate
ma	to give
gyina	to stand / stop
anim [ænim]	front (from ani : eye / surface; mu : inside)
edan	building / room
efie	house / home
nsesa	change (n); from sesa: to change/give change

39

EXERCISE

Make up a short dialogue between you and a taxi driver, using some of the expressions you have learnt in this lesson.

Dialogue 12

Kofi: Mary, worekɔ hě na w'ani abere sei?	Mary, where are you going that (and) you look so harrassed (your eyes are so red)?
Mary: Merekɔ Nkran.	I'm going to Accra.
Merekɔtotɔ nneɛma pii.	I'm going to buy many things.
Merepɛ ntɛm paa.	I'm in a great hurry.
Kofi: Kɔfa taksi ɛ?	(why don't you) Go and take a taxi?
ɛha deɛ, wonya [wunya] kaa ntɛm.	Here, you won't get a vehicle quickly.
Mary: Taksi bɛgye sika pii.	A taxi will charge (take) a lot of money.
Taksi boɔ yɛ den dodo.	Taxis are (taxi price is) too expensive.
Mɛtwɛn trɔtrɔ.	I'll wait for a 'trɔ trɔ'.
Kofi: ɛnneɛ wompɛ ntɛm pii.	Well, you can't be in a great hurry.
Mary: Me sika sua, enti a.	My money is small, that is why.
Kofi: ɛyɛ me sɛ	It (is) seems to me that
bɔs wei rekɔ [ɛɛkɔ] Nkran.	this bus is going to Accra.
ɛkwan baakő aka wɔ mu.	There is one place left in it.
Kɔtena mu kɔ.	Go and take it (go sit in it & go).
Mɛnya [menya] foforɔ.	I will get another (new) one.
Mary: Yoo. Medaase.	All right. Thank you.
Akyire yi yɛbɛhyia.	See you later. (Later we'll meet.)

Vocabulary

bere	to be red
totɔ	to buy (with plural object)
nneɛma	things
adeɛ	thing
kaa	any vehicle / car
ntɛm	quickly
pɛ ntɛm	to be in a hurry
twɛn	to wait

40

ɛkwan	way / road / space
tena	to sit
nya	to obtain
foforɔ	new / another
trɔtrɔ	mini buses that operate within towns/cities (from trɔ : threepence, the original minimum fare on such vehicles)

Grammar points

1. sɛ : that

eg.
Mepɛ sɛ mekɔ.	I want to go (I want that I go).
ɔkaa sɛ ɔbɛba.	S/he said that s/he will come.
ɛyɛ me sɛ ɔbɛba.	I think (it seems to me) that s/he'll come.
Menim sɛ ɔbɛyɛ.	I know that s/he will do it.

2. totɔ : to buy (with plural object)
Verb stems may be doubled (or repeated) to indicate a plural subject or object, to indicate repeated action or to have a slight change in the meaning of the verb. This is called reduplication, and is discussed further in Lesson 26. A few examples are given here.

Bisa no.	Ask him/her.
Bisebisa wɔn.	Ask them.
Dua bi si hɔ.	(There is) a tree standing there.
Nnua pii sisi hɔ.	There are many trees standing there.
Bu mu.	Break it (once).
Bubu mu.	Keep breaking it into many pieces.
Hwɛ.	Look at it.
Hwehwɛ.	Look for it.

3. Mɛnya [menya] foforɔ.
When the vowel a occurs with certain consonants, as in gya, nya, twa, dwa, the vowels that occur in the prefixes are from Group 2: i e o u

eg.
ɔbɛgya [obegya].	She will leave it behind.
Yɛbɛnya [yebenya].	We will get it.
Metwa [mitwa].	I cut it.
Wodware [wudware] ha.	You have your bath here.
Onyame	God
odwan	sheep
egya	fire/firewood

EXERCISE

Express the following sentences in Twi, using the conjunction 'sε'. Make up others of your own.

S/he wants to come.
I know that s/he will go to Accra.
It seems to me that s/he is eating.
Kofi knows I like football.
You want to go.
S/he knows I will come.

LESSON 10

GIVING DIRECTIONS

Dialogue 13

John: Kofi, maahâ.	Good afternoon, Kofi.
Kofi: Yaa asɔn. ɛte sɛn?	(response) How is it?
John: Bɔkɔɔ. Na wo nso ɛ?	Fine (soft). And you?
Kofi: Me nso me hõ yɛ.	I'm also fine.
Na ɛha yi ɛ?	What are you doing here? (And here too?)
John: ɔpanyin sikani [sikæni] bi te ha baabi [bææbi].	A certain rich man lives around here.
M'adamfo yi rehwehwɛ [yiihwehwɛ] no.	This friend of mine is looking for him
Kofi: ɔpanyin [ɔpænyin] Yaw Poku?	Opanyin (elder) Yaw Poku?
John: Aane. Wonim ne fiee?	Yes. Do you know his house?
Kofi: ɛwɔ abrɔsan fitaa no akyi.	It is behind the white two storey building.
Kɔ w'anim têê.	Go straight ahead (in front of you).
Wodu nkwanta no so a, fa nifa.	When you get to the junction, turn (take) right.
Wobɛhû sɛ abrɔsan no si benkum so wɔ ɛkwan no hõ.	You will see that the two storey building is on the left near the street.
Fitia kɛseɛ bi si abrɔsan no akyi.	A big single storey (short) house stands behind the two storey building.
ɛhɔ na Agya Yaw Poku te(ɛ).	That is where 'father' Yaw Poku lives
John: Yoo. Medaase.	OK. Thank you.
ɛnneɛ me ne no rekɔ [nookɔ] aba.	Well then, I'm going with him (I and him are going) and we'll be back.
Yɛbɛba seesei ara.	We'll be back very soon.
Kofi: Yoo.	OK.
Mmɛhwɛ mo anim.	I'll expect you (plu).

43

Vocabulary

ɔpanyin [ɔpænyin]	elder . The title usually refers to men; for women, : ɔbaa panyin, i.e. female elder).
mpanyimfoɔ	elders (for both men and women)
(o)sikani	a rich person (sika: money; oni: person)
baabi [bææbi]	somewhere (bea : place; bi : a certain)
ɔhɔhoɔ	stranger / visitor
hwehwɛ	to look for / search (reduplicated from hwɛ : look)
abrɔsan	2/3 or more storey building (from borɔ: foreign; dan: building)
akyi(re)	the back
tɛ̌ɛ̌	straight ahead
du(ru)	reach / arrive at
nkwanta	junction (ɔkwan : road; ata : twin/double)
nkwantanan	crossroads; i.e. a four-way junction
(ɛ)so	on (the top / surface of) see 'postpositions' below.
nifǎ	right
benkum	left
si	to be standing (used of trees, houses, vehicles etc.)
fitia	short house / single storey building (from fie : house; tia : short)
tia	short.
akwatia	short person (akoa : fellow; tia : short)
te	to reside in a place
bra / ba	to come. It is 'bra' in the imperative positive, but 'ba' in all other forms of the verb.

eg.

Bra!	Come!	ɔmmra!	Let him come!
Meba.	I come.	ɔbɛba.	He will come.
Yɛbae.	We came.	Mma!	Don't come!

Grammar points

1. 'Prepositions' : The equivalent of English prepositions are nouns which occur after other nouns, and therefore sometimes called 'postpositions', as illustrated below:

aseɛ :	the under part	ɔpon no ase:	under the table
ɛso :	the top	ɔpon no so :	on top of the table
akyi(re) :	the back	ɛdan no akyi:	behind the house

anim :	front (face)	ɛdan no anim:	in front of the house
ɛhõ :	outside (body)	ɛdan no hõ:	outside the building
(e)mu :	inside	adaka no mu:	inside the box

2. a : subordinate clause marker, as in

Wodu nkwanta no so a ...	When you reach the junction ...
Sɛ ɔba a ...	If s/he comes ...
Abofra a ɔbaa ha no ...	The child who came here ...
Bere a mekɔɔ hɔ no ...	When (the time that) I went there...

(In the last two examples 'a' is a relative clause marker.)

EXERCISE

1. Give directions to where you live.
2. Select the correct 'preposition' to complete the following sentences:

ɛda ɔpon no _____.	It is on the table.
ɔgyina ɛdan no _____.	S/he's standing in font of the house.
ɛwɔ adaka no _____.	It is behind the box.
ɔwɔ sukuu dan no _____.	S/he's inside the school building.
ɔgyina dua no _____.	S/he's standing under the tree.

45

Lesson 11

FOOD

Dialogue 14

Mary :	Agoo!	'Knocking'
Amma :	Amee. Hwan a?	(response) Who is it?
Mary :	ɛyɛ me Mary.	It is me, Mary.
Amma :	Mary, bra mu.	Mary, come in.
Mary :	Amma, ɛkɔm de me paa.	Amma, I'm very hungry (hunger has taken hold of me).
	Wowɔ aduane?	Do you have food?
Amma :	Aane, mewɔ paanoo;	Yes, I have bread;
	mewɔ aborɔbɛ nso.	I also have pineapple.
Mary :	Wonni aduane papa wɔ hɔ?	Don't you have real / proper food?
Amma :	Mewɔ ɛmo ne frɔeɛ wɔ hɔ.	I have rice and stew (there).
	Mɛka no hye ama wo.	I will warm it for (give) you.
Mary :	ɛbɛkyɛre.	It will take long.
	Merepɛ ntɛm.	I'm in a hurry.
	Mɛdi [medi] paanoo no.	I will eat the bread.
	Wowɔ nsuo?	Do you have water?
	Sukɔm de me paa.	I'm very thirsty (thirst has taken hold of me).
Amma :	Mewɔ nsuo wɔ hɔ.	I have water (there).
	Mewɔ tii nso.	I also have tea.
	Wopɛ paanoo ne tii anaasɛ wopɛ paanoo ne nsuo?	Do you want bread and tea or do you want bread and water?
Mary :	Mepɛ paanoo ne tii.	I want bread and tea.
	Yɛ tii no bi ma me.	Make some of the tea for me.
Amma :	ɛno ni.	Here it is.
Mary :	Medaase pii.	Thank you very much.
	Mamee paa.	I am very full.
Amma :	Yɛnni aseda / aseda nni mu.	You don't owe me thanks.
Mary :	ɛnneɛ merekɔ.	(Well) then, I'm leaving.
Amma :	Yoo. Yɛbɛhyia.	OK. See you (we'll meet).

Vocabulary

ɛkɔm	hunger
aduane	food
paanoo	bread (also: brodo)

46

aborɔbɛ	pineapple (borɔ: foreign; abɛ: palm bunch)
ɛmo	rice
frɔeɛ	stew / sauce
pɛ ntɛm	to be in a hurry (pɛ: want; ntɛm: quick / fast)
nom	to drink
nsuo	water
sukɔm	thirst (nsu(o): water; (ɛ)kɔm: hunger)
anaasɛ	or
mee	to be full / to have eaten enough

Other common food items

asikyire	sugar
kosua	egg (nkosua: eggs)
ɛnam	meat / fish (i.e. flesh)
nsuomnam	fish ('flesh from water')
nantwinam	beef (nantwie: cow; nam: flesh)
akokɔnam	chicken (akokɔ: chicken, i.e. the animal)
dwanam	lamb / mutton (odwan: sheep)
prakonam	pork (prako: pig)
nkyene	salt
mako	pepper
gyeene	onion(s)
ɛnkwan	soup
nkatenkwan	groundnut soup (nkateɛ: groundnuts/peanuts)
abɛnkwan	palmnut soup (abɛ: palm nuts)
nkaakra	light/pepper soup
fufuo	fufu (boiled cassava, plantain, or yam that is pounded and eaten with soup)
kelewele	fried ripe plantain
apesie	boiled yam, plantain, or cocoyam eaten with sauce/stew
borɔdeɛ	plantain
kɔkɔɔ	ripe plantain
adua	beans
dɔkono	kenkey (made from corn/maize dough)
banku	banku (also made from corn dough)
anwâ	vegetable oil
ɛngo	palm oil
sradeɛ	(animal) fat

Grammar points

The verb 'de' (to take) is used to express certain sensations.
eg. Ɛkɔm de me.　　　　　I'm hungry
　　　　　　　　　　　　(hunger has taken {hold of} me).

47

Sukɔm de me (paa).	I'm (very) thirsty.
Awɔ de me.	I'm cold (awɔ: cold weather).
Ahuhuro de yɛn.	We are feeling hot.
	(ahuhuro: hot sticky weather)
Dwonsɔ de no.	S/he wants to 'pee'. (dwonsɔ: urine)

Dialogue 15

Amma:	Abenaa, maahã.	Abenaa, good afternoon.
Abenaa:	Yaa nua.	(response)
	ɛte sɛn?	How is it?
Amma:	Onyame adom, ɛyɛ.	By God's grace, fine.
	Na wo nso ɛ?	And you?
Abenaa:	Me nso me hõ yɛ.	I'm also fine.
Amma:	Yɛda Onyame ase.	We thank God.
	Na worekɔ hẽ awia yi?	And where are you going this afternoon?
Abenaa:	Merekɔ edwa mu.	I'm going to the market.
	Merekɔpɛ aduane atɔ.	I'm going to look for food to buy.
Amma:	Adɛn wonni aduane wɔ fie?	Why, don't you have food at home?
Abenaa:	Aane, menni hwee wɔ fie.	Yes, I don't have anything at home.
	Me nam asa, enti merekɔpɛ nantwinam atɔ.	My meat / fish is finished, so I'm going to look for beef to buy.
	Menni bayerɛ anaasɛ ɛmo mpo.	I don't have yam or rice even.
	Me ba ketewa no nso pɛ kɔkɔɔ, enti mɛtɔ bi.	My little child also likes ripe plantain, so I'll buy some.
Amma:	Na ankaa ne kwadu [kwædu] nso ɛ?	And how about oranges and bananas?
	Wowɔ bi?	Do you have any?
Abenaa:	Daabi [dææbi].	No.
Amma:	Mewɔ ankaa ne kwadu pii wɔ fie.	I have plenty of oranges and bananas at home.
	Bɛgye bi kɔma wo ba no.	Come and get some for (go give) your child.
Abenaa:	Medaase.	Thank you.
	Mɛba abɛgye.	I'll come for (and get) them.
Amma:	ɛnneɛ kɔ edwa mu bra.	Well then, go to the market and come.
	Merekɔnoa aduane.	I'm going to cook (food).

48

Mɛtwɛn wo wɔ fie.   I'll wait for you at home.
Abenaa: Yoo, merekɔ aba.   OK. I'll be back.
                                (I'm going and will come.)

Vocabulary

edwa	market
pɛ	look for
bayerɛ	yam
hwee	nothing
enti	and so / therefore
ketewa	little / small
bi	some / any
noa	to cook / boil

Some common food items in the market

mankani	cocoyam
kontomire	spinach / cocoyam leaves
akatewa / agusi	seeds of a type of melon, used in cooking kontomire
bankye	cassava / manioc
gari	processed cassava
ankaa	orange(s)
ankaa twadeɛ	lime
borɔferɛ	pawpaw / papaya
aburoo	maize / corn
nyaadoa	garden eggs / egg plant
tomatos / ntoosi	tomatoes

Grammar points

Amma: Don't you have food in the house?
Abenaa: Yes, I don't have anything in the house.

In English, Abenaa's response would have started with 'No'. In Akan, the answer 'Yes' or 'No' is in response to the question, i.e. agreeing (yes) or disagreeing (no) with the question, as illustrated by the two questions and answers below.

i. A: Wo papa wɔ fie?   Is your father at home?
    B: Daabi.   No.
       (Me papa nni fie)   (My father is not at home.)
ii. A: Wo papa nni fie?   Isn't your father at home?
    B: Aane.   Yes.
       (Me papa nni fie)   (My father is not at home.)

49

Express the folowing sentences in Twi:
I am going to the market.
I will buy eggs and beef.
I will also buy ripe plantain and one yam.
I don't have oranges, so I will buy some.
I have garden eggs, salt and onions so I won't buy any.
I buy bread everyday, so I have some at home.

Dialogue 16

Kofi:	Kɔkɔɔkɔ.	Knocking.
Amma:	Bra mu.	Come in.
Kofi:	Amma, maahǎ.	Amma, good afternoon.
Amma:	Yaa nua.	(response)
	Akonnwa nie.	Here's a chair.
Kofi:	Medaase.	Thank you.
	Na wo hɔ̃ te sɛn?	And how are you?
Amma:	Me hɔ̃ yɛ. Na wo nso ɛ?	I'm fine. And you too?
Kofi:	Me nso me hɔ̃ yɛ.	I'm also well.
Amma:	Yɛda Onyame ase.	We thank God.
	Na awia [æwia] yi ɛ?	And this afternoon?
		(i.e. What brings you here?)
Kofi:	Bɔkɔɔ.	Soft, i.e. nothing amiss.
	Mebɛsraa wo.	I came to visit you.
	Mehũũ wo akyɛ.	It's a long time since I saw you.
Amma:	Woayɛ [wayɛ] adeɛ.	You've done well.
	ɛdeɛn na wobɛnom, Fanta, Coca Cola anaasɛ bia?	What will you drink, Fanta, Coca Cola or beer?
Kofi:	Coca Cola yɛ.	Coca Cola is fine.
Amma:	ɛnneɛ mewɔ keek(i), mɛtwa [metwa] bi akǎ hɔ̃.	Well then I have some cake, I'll cut some and add it.
	ɛno ni.	Here it is.
Kofi:	Medaase. ɛnneɛ me nsa akǎ.	Thank you. Well, I've got (my hands have touched) something.
Amma:	Yoo, kɔ so.	All right, go ahead.
	Kofi, woakɔsra [wakɔsra] wo maame nnansǎ yi?	Kofi, have you been (gone) to visit your mother recently (these three days)?
Kofi:	Aane. Mekɔɔ hɔ ɛnnɛ ne nnaawɔtwe.	Yes. I went there a week today. (today is one week)

	Makɔ hɔ mprɛnsâ bosome yi mu.	I've been there three times this month (inside this month)
	Me maame deɛ, metaa sra no.	As for my mother, I visit her often.
Amma:	Mo, saa na ɛyɛ. Woyɛ adeɛ paa. Na ne hõ te sɛn?	Well done, that is good (as it should be). You do very well. And how is she?
Kofi:	Ne hõ yɛ. Amma, wo keeki no yɛ dɛ paa.	She is well. Amma, your cake is very nice.
	Medaase pii.	Thank you very much.
	Mɛsrɛ kwan akɔ.	I'll ask permission to leave.
Amma:	Yoo, ɛkwan da hɔ.	All right. The way is clear.
	Medaase ne nsra.	Thank you for the visit.

Vocabulary

akonnwa / adwa	chair
nkonnwa	chairs
awia	sun / afternoon
bɔkɔɔ	soft i.e. everything is fine / all is well
me nsa akâ	I've (my hand has) received (something) (nsa : hand; kâ: to touch)
sra	to pay a visit
nsra	visit (noun)
akyɛ(re)	it's been a long time
mprɛnsâ	three times (mprɛ: times; mmeɛnsâ: 3)
prɛkõ	once (prɛ: time; {baa}kõ: one)
mprenu	twice (mprɛ: times; {mmie}nu: two)
mprɛnan	four times
deɛ	emphatic particle, 'as for ...'
taa	often
yɛ adeɛ	to do something (admirable)
srɛ	to beg / plead
(ɛ)kwan	road / way
srɛ kwan	to ask permission to go somewhere
ɛkwan da hɔ	permission is granted (the way is clear)

Grammar points

1. Note the Perfect verbs in the dialogue:

woayɛ [wayɛ] (adeɛ)	you've done (well)
(me nsa) aka	(my hand) has received
woakɔsra [wakɔsra]	have you been (gone) to visit ..
makɔ	I have gone ...

51

2. deɛ : emphatic particle
   This is commonly used with nouns (or pronouns), usually at the beginning of a sentence.

Kofi deɛ, ɔmpɛ fufuo.	As for Kofi, he doesn't like fufu.
Adwuma yi deɛ, ɛyɛ den paa.	As for this job, it is very difficult.
Ne nnwomtoɔ deɛ, ɛsɛ w'asɔ.	As for his/her singing, you must hear it.
Yɛn deɛ, yɛmpene so.	We (emphatic) don't agree.

Note that in these sentences, the subject pronoun occurs with the verb even when there is a noun subject.

3. taa : often
   This behaves like a verb, occurring with the pronoun subject and inflecting for the negative.

Kofi taa ba ha.	Kofi often comes here.
Amma ntaa mma ha.	Amma does not come here often.
Metaa hũ no.	I often see him/her.
Mentaa nhũ wo.	I don't see you often.

Note that in the negative sentences, the negative prefix occurs before both 'taa' and the main verb.

EXERCISE

Make up four sentences each with the words 'deɛ' and 'taa'.

Culture points

1. Amma is at home when Kofi calls. She therefore asks him to sit down 'akonnwa nie' (here's a chair) before they ask after each other's health.
2. When you visit someone at home or in the office, it is normal for the person to ask the reason for the visit, referred to as 'amaneɛ' (i.e. your mission), even when s/he knows why you are there.
   Amma asks : 'Awia yi ɛ?' i.e.   What brings you here this afternoon?
   She could also have asked: 'Amaneɛ?'
3. It is also normal to offer a visitor something to drink. Usually it is a glass of water to quench his/her thirst, since s/he may have walked some distance in the sun to get to your house. This is usually done before the 'amaneɛ'. In this dialogue, Amma knows Kofi very well, and she knows he has not travelled a long distance to visit her, and so asks the 'amaneɛ' before offering him a drink.

4. It is also part of the culture to invite people to share one's food, so Kofi tells Amma 'Me nsa akã.', even though it is Amma who gave him the food in the first place. Amma turns down the offer with 'Kɔ so.' (Go ahead).

5. Note the expressions for asking and granting leave.

   Kofi :   Mɛsrɛ kwan. I'll ask permission to leave.
   Amma :   ɔkwan da hɔ. The way is clear / you're free to go.

Lesson 12

THE FAMILY

Dialogue 17

Kofi: Mary, maakyε.	Good morning, Mary.
Adεn na w'ani agye sei?	Why are you so happy?
Mary: Kofi, yaa nua.	(response)
εnnε deε m'ani agye paa.	As for today I'm very happy.
Me nsa akã krataa afi [æfi] me	I have received letters from
nuanom mmienu hɔ.	two of my brothers & sisters.
Wɔɔnom / ɔɔmo wɔ	They are overseas.
aburokyire.	
Kofi: Saa? Wo nuanom sεn na εwɔ	Is that so? How many of
aburokyire?	your brothers & sisters are
	overseas?
Mary: Wɔɔnom yε εnan; ɔbaa	There are four of them;
baakõ εna mmarima mmeεnsã.	one woman (female) and
	three men (male).
Kofi: Se/sε moyε enum pε? Enti wo	Aren't there only five of
nuanom nyinaa wɔ aburokyire?	you? So are all your
	siblings abroad?
Mary: Aane. Me nkõãã na mewɔ	Yes. I am the only one in
Ghana.	(I alone am in) Ghana.
Kofi: Na Akosua ε?	And how about Akosua?
ɔnyε wo nua?	Isn't she your sister?
Mary: Oo, ɔyε me nua.	Oh (yes), she is my sister
	(cousin).
ɔyε me maame nua ba.	She is the daughter of my
	mother's sister.
Kofi: Saa? Me deε menim	Is that so? I (emphatic)
sε ɔyε wo maame ne wo papa	thought she is the child of
ba.	your mother and father.
Na Kwame ne Kofi nso ε?	And how about Kwame and
	Kofi?
Mary: Kwame yε me wɔfa ba, εna	Kwame is my uncle's son, and
Kofi nso yε me papa kumaa	Kofi is my 'younger' father's
ba.	(i.e. my father's younger
	brother's) son.
Kofi: Moyε nua ma εyε fε.	The way you carry on like
	brothers and sisters is nice.

54

Woakɔsra aburokyirefoɔ no pɛn anaa?	Have you gone to visit the overseas people before?
Mary: Daabi. Menni tikit sika.	No, I don't have money for the ticket.
Kofi: Ka kyerɛ wɔɔnom na wɔmfa tikit mmrɛ wo.	Tell them to bring you a ticket.
Mary: Yoo. Merekɔ fie akɔtwerɛ wɔɔnom seesei ara.	All right. I'm going home right now to write to them.
Kofi: Ka kyerɛ wɔɔnom sɛ mekyea wɔn.	Tell them I greet them.
Mary: Yoo, mɛka akyerɛ wɔn.	OK. I'll tell them.

Vocabulary

sei (sɛ eyi)	like this
nsa akâ	to receive (hand has touched)
krataa	letter / paper
se / sɛ	question word meaning 'isn't it true that?'
nkôâ	only
kumaa	younger / smaller
aburokyirefoɔ	people living abroad
twerɛ	to write

Kinship terms

Singular		Plural
maame/ɛna/ eno	mother/adult female (also female relative of one's mother)	maamenom / ɛnanom/enonom
papa/agya	father/adult male (also male relative of one's father)	papanom / agyanom
nua	sibling (brother/sister/cousin)	(a)nuanom
nuabaa	sister/female cousin	nuanom mmaa
nuabarima [nuabɛɛma]	brother/male cousin	nuanom mmarima [mmɛɛma]
nana	grandparent	nananom (also 'ancestors')
yere	wife	yerenom
kunu	husband (also male relative of husband)	kununom
kunu panyin	husband's elder brother	
kunu kumaa	husband's younger brother	
ɔba	child	mma
ɔba baa	daughter	mma mmaa

ɔba barima [bɛɛma]	son	mma mmarima [mmɛɛma]
wɔfa	uncle (mother's brother/male cousin)	wɔfanom
wɔfaase	neice/nephew; child of a man's sister	wɔfaasenom
sewaa	aunt (father's sister/ female cousin)	sewaanom
aseɛ	father / mother-in-law son / daughter-in-law	nsenom
akumaa	sister-in-law	nkumaafoɔ
akonta	brother-in-law	nkotanom
abusũã	(extended) family	

Grammar points

1. Kinship nouns usually form their plural by adding the suffix '-nom', as can be seen from the above examples.

2. nkõãã (only) always implies that there is an expectation of a bigger number or quantity.

eg. Kofi nkõãã na ɔyɛɛ adwuma no.
It is Kofi only who did the work.
Wo nkõãã kɔfa bra.   You alone go and bring (take come) it.
Mmofra no nkõãã na aba. It is only the children who are here.

Culture points

1. Asantes and all Akans have the extended family system, in which the family (abusũã [æbuswiã]) includes a mother and her children as well as all maternal aunts and uncles, and all maternal cousins and grandparents. Akans have a matrilineal system in which lineage is traced through the mother. All members of the 'abusũã' are ultimately descended from one woman.
2. Twi does not have a word for cousin, the word for sibling, 'nuá' [nwiã] is used.
3. Mother's sisters and father's brothers are all referred to as mothers and fathers respectively.
4. The word for neice / nephew refers only to children of a man's sister. A man refers to his brother's child as his child 'ɔba'. A woman also refers to her sister's child as her 'ɔba'.

EXERCISE

1. Express the following in Asante
   I have five brothers and sisters: three girls and two boys.
   My mother's sister is in Kumasi.
   My uncle (mother's brother) is a student in Britain.
   My uncle (father's brother) is a teacher.
   I don't have a sister, I have two brothers.
   My aunt (father's sister) lives in Washington.

2. Talk / write about your family.

Lesson 13

CLOTHES

Dialogue 18

Kofi: Amma maadwo.
Woreko hɛ anwumere yi?

Good evening, Amma.
Where are you going this evening?

Amma: Kofi, yaa nua.
Mereko paati. Abenaa redi [eedi] n'awoda nnɛ.

(response)
I'm going to a party. Abenaa is celebrating her birthday today.

Kofi: Ei saa? Wadi mfeɛ sɛn?

Really? How old is she?

Amma: Wadi mfeɛ aduonu baakõ.
Mekyɛn no afe.

She is twenty one years old.
I am one year older than her.

Kofi: Wo hõ ayɛ fɛ paa.
Wo ntoma yi fata wo paa.

You look very pretty.
Your cloth (i.e. traditional long skirt and top) looks very nice on you.

Amma: Medaase. Me maame kumaa na ɔpam maa me.

Thank you. It is my aunt (mother's younger sister) who sewed it for me.

Kofi: Wo maame no nim adeɛ pam paa. Kaba no fata wo paa.

That aunt knows how to sew very well. The top suits you very well.

Amma, wopɛ laif!

Amma, you like life (you're fashion-conscious).

W'asomaadeɛ ne kɔnmuadeɛ yi yɛ soronkõ.
Na adɛn nti na wohyɛ ahenemma yi?
Wo mpaboa wɔ hɛ?

Your earings and necklace are really special.
But why are you wearing these open sandals?
Where are your shoes?

Amma: Me nansoa ahon, enti mentumi nhyɛ mpaboa.

My toe is swollen, therefore I can't wear shoes.

Kofi: Kosɛ, enneɛ wontumi nsa wɔ Abenaa paati no ase.

Sorry. That means you can't dance at Abenaa's party.

Amma: Aane, nanso mɛgye m'ani paa. Mɛdidi [medidi] na manom. Me ne me nnamfo nso bɛdi nkɔmɔ asere.

Yes, but I will enjoy myself very well. I will eat and drink. I will also chat and laugh with my friends.

Kofi: Wokɔ a mekyea Abenaa.

When you go give Abenaa my regards (greet her for me)

Kā kyerɛ no sɛ mema ne tiri nkwā.	Tell her I congratulate her (I give her head {long} life).
Amma: Mɛkā akyerɛ no.	I'll tell her.
Yɛbɛhyia bio.	We'll meet again.
Baabaae.	Goodbye.

Vocabulary

awoda	birthday (wo: give birth; da: day)
di awoda	to celebrate a birthday
kyɛn	(greater / better) than
ntoma/ntama	cloth (usually used to refer to traditional outfit for men and for women)
pam	to sew
kaba	top part of women's outfit (from 'cover' of the original expression 'cover shoulder')
pɛ laif	to like life / to be fashion conscious
hyɛ	to wear (accessories and Western clothes)
ahenemma/ kyawkyaw	Asante leather sandals; also called 'kyawkyaw' because of the noise they make when one walks in them.
mpaboa	shoes / sandals
asomaadeɛ	earrings (asô: ear; mu: inside; adeɛ: thing)
kɔnmuadeɛ	necklace (kɔn: neck; mu: inside; adeɛ: thing)
soronkô	special / unusual / unique
kosɛ	sorry (expression of sympathy)
ase(ɛ)	the base of (here used as a preposition : at the party)
nom	to drink
nnamfo	friends
adamfo	friend
di nkɔmɔ	to converse (di: to eat; nkɔmɔ: conversation)
sere	to laugh
tiri nkwā	congratulations (tiri: head; nkwā: life)

Other common items of clothing

akatasoɔ	second piece of cloth of the female outfit used to tie up a baby on its mother's back; now often used as headtie
duku	head scarf
ataadeɛ	dress; usually Western outfit
kente	kente: colourful hand-woven cloth
kawa/koa	ring
ɛkyɛ	hat

kyale wɔtee	foam sandals / flip-flops
	('Charlie let's go' in the Gã language)
pieto	underpants
bɔdis	brassiere
batakari/	loose toga made with handwoven cotton;
fuugu	traditional outfit of men in the northern part of the country.

Notes

1. There are two verbs meaning 'to wear' used with different items of clothing and accessories.

   a) fura: to wear or wrap around a piece of cloth as usually done in a typical Ghanaian outfit.

Kofi fura kente / ntoma.	Kofi is wearing kente / cloth.
Amma fura ntoma.	Amma is wearing/has on Ghanaian outfit.
Ne kaba no yɛ fɛ paa.	Her kaba is very beautiful.
Ne slit no sua; ɛkye no.	Her slit (long fitting skirt worn with 'kaba') is small; it is tight on her.
Ne ntoma no yɛ 'Dumas'.	Her cloth (material) is wax print. (Dumas was the man who first sold wax prints in Ghana.)
Yɛfrɛ no akyekyedeɛ akyi.	It is called the back (akyi) of a tortoise (akyekyedeɛ). (the motif in it is the shell of a tortoise).

   b) hyɛ: to wear, usually Western or close fitting outfit such as the slit or kaba, so that a woman in Ghanaian outfit may be spoken of in two different ways:

ɔfura [ofura] ntoma.	She is wearing cloth.
OR ɔhyɛ slit ne kaba.	She is wearing slit and kaba.

   'hyɛ' is the only verb used for accessories such as hats, earrings, shoes, as in:

Kofi hyɛ kawa / koa.	Kofi has a ring on.
Mary hyɛ asomaade fɛɛfɛ bi.	Mary is wearing (some) beautiful earrings.

2. kyɛn / sen : than

   These two words are used in comparative expressions:

i. Kofi ware kyɛn / sen wo.	Kofi is taller than you.
ii. Kofi kyɛn wo tenten.	Kofi passes you in height.
iii. Amma nim adeɛ kyɛn / sen me.	Amma is more clever than me.
iv. Amma kyɛn me wɔ adesũã mu.	Amma is more clever than me (passes me in learning).

v. Wei sua kyɛn/sen baakõ no.   This is smaller than that one.
vi. Wei nsua nkyɛn/nsen baakõ no.   This isn't smaller than that one.
vii. Amma nnim adeɛ nkyɛn/nsen me.

Amma isn't more clever than me.

viii. Amma nkyɛn me wɔ adesua mu.

Amma isn't more clever than me.

Note that
a) 'kyɛn' is used on its own as a verb to mean 'greater than' in sentences (ii) and (iv).
b) 'sen' can also be used in the same context, but 'kyɛn' is the word that is usually preferred.
c) Both 'kyɛn' and 'sen' on their own imply a greater or better quality. It is therefore not possible to use 'kyɛn' on its own as an alternative to sentence (v) where the item is smaller.

'Wei kyɛn baakõ no.' can only mean :
This one is bigger / better than that one.

In sentences (vi) to (viii) these words are in the negative. Like verbs, they occur with the negative prefix 'n-'.

Grammar points

1. The verb 'di' (to eat) combines with various words to express a variety of meanings.

eg. di awoda   to have/celebrate a birthday
    di nkɔmɔ   to have a chat/conversation
    di asɛm   to settle/judge a case
    di bem   to win a case
    'di' plus time word   used to express time or age
    di bosome   to spend a month (in a place)
    wadi mfeɛ du   s/he is ten years old

2. The verb 'ma' (to give) often translates as the preposition 'for' when used with other verbs.

eg. ɔpam maa me.   S/he sewed it for me.
    Kyea no ma me.   Greet him/her for me.
    Frɛ no ma me.   Call him/her for me.

3. aseɛ (the base / bottom of) also translates as the preposition 'under' or 'at' depending on the noun it occurs after. (see also 'Prepositions' Lessons 10 and 33)

eg. paati no ase   at the party
    nhyiamu no ase   at the meeting
    ɔpon no ase   under the table
    mpa no ase   under the bed

61

Culture points

Wo tiri nkwǎ. Congratulations! ({long} life to your head).
Me tiri da ase. Thank you (my head thanks you).

This is used on occasions such as birthdays, the birth of
a child, on getting married, on passing an examination, on
getting a job or any such happy occasion.

Mo! : well done/congratulations! will not be appropriate
in this context since it is used when somebody has actually
done something admirable.

Lesson 14

THE BODY

Dialogue 19

Kofi:	Agoo	Knocking.
Mary:	Amee	(response)
Kofi:	Mary maahã	Good afternoon, Mary.
Mary:	Yaa nua. ɛte sɛn?	(response) How is it?
Kofi:	ɛyɛ, na wo nso ɛ?	Fine, and how about you?
Mary:	Aa, ɛyɛ.	Ah, I'm fine.
Kofi:	Adɛn, woyare anaa?	Why, are you ill?
Mary:	Aane. Me ti yɛ me ya.	Yes. My head is aching.
	Awɔ nso de me.	I'm also feverish (I'm cold).
Kofi:	Oo, kosɛ. Woahũ dɔkta?	Oh, sorry. Have you seen a doctor?
Mary:	Daabi. Me nan, mentumi nsɔre nkɔ baabiara.	No. My legs, I cannot get up to go anywhere.
Kofi:	Mede kaa bae.	I came in a car.
	Sɔre na yɛnkɔhũ [yenkohũ] dɔkta.	Get up and let us go to see a doctor.
	ɔbɛma wo aduro.	S/he'll give you medicine.
	Wo ti ne wo nan ne wo hõnam ɛnyɛ wo ya bio.	Your head and your legs and your body won't hurt anymore (again).
Mary:	Medaase pii.	Thank you very much.
	Onyame nhyira wo.	God bless you.

Vocabulary

yare	to be sick
yɛ ya	to hurt / be painful
tumi	to be able
nan	leg(s)
sɔre	to get up
aduro	medicine
hõnam	the muscles of the body (hõ: body; nam: flesh)
hyira	to bless

Other parts of the body

eti(re)	head	ani / aniwa	eye(s)

63

atikɔ	back of the head	ani kosua	eye ball (egg)
adwene	brain	ani ntɔn	eyebrow (bow)
(e)nwi	hair	anisua tɛtɛ	eye lashes
ti nwi	hair on the head		(tears are suspended
mfemfem	moustache		on them)
moma	forehead	anim	face
asŏ	ear	afono	cheek(s)
kɔn	neck	hwene	nose
koko	chest	ano	mouth/lips
nufoɔ	breast(s)	anom(u)	mouth (inside)
mfɛ̃	rib cage	tɛkrɛma	tongue
akoma	heart	mene	throat
basa	arm	(ɛ)sɛ̃	tooth/teeth
bati	shoulder	abɔdwe	jaw/chin
bakɔn	wrist	abɔdwesɛ	beard
yafunu/	stomach	nsa	arm/hand
yam(u)		nsatɛ̃ãã	finger(s)
ayaaseɛ	lower abdomen	nsam(u)	palm
funuma	navel	nan tabono	feet (leg oar)
ɛtoɔ	buttocks	nantuo	calf (leg gun)
serɛ	thigh(s)	kotodwe	knee
akyi	back	nantini	heel

Note: The expression 'yɛ' (to be) 'ya' (painful) is used to express physical pain, as in the above dialogue. It may also be used to express regret, as in the following examples:

ɛyɛ me ya sɛ worekɔ.	I am sorry that you are leaving.
ɛyɛ no ya sɛ woanhũ no.	S/he is sorry you didn't see him/her. (i.e. s/he was out)

Grammar points

1. Mary says she cannot go to any place:

me-n-tumi	n-sɔre	n-kɔ
I-not-can	not-get up	not-go

It has already been pointed out that these are serial verb constructions (Lesson 7, Dialogue 7). When the sentence is in the negative, all the verbs occur in the negative, as illustrated above.

Other examples:

n-kɔfa kaa no m-ma.	Don't go and bring (take come) the car.
ɔ-m-fa n-kyerɛ no.	S/he won't (take) show it to him/her.

2. The verb 'tumi' (to be able) often occurs as the first verb in serial verb constructions.

eg. Metumi sɔre ntɛm.   I am able to get up early.
    Yɛtumi kɔsra no wɔ sukuu.   We can visit him/her at school.
    Wotumi ba bɛgye.   You can come and collect it.

Give the negative of these sentences.

3. Onyame nhyira wo. : May God bless you.

The Optative form of the verb has a prefix m- or n-. The whole verb is also pronounced on a high pitch. It may be preceded by an optional 'ma' (let).

eg. ɔnkɔda.   Let him/her go and sleep.
    (ma) Yɛmfrɛ no.   Let us call him/her.
    (ma) ɔnka n'asɛm.   Let him/her tell his/her (side of the)
                         story.

(See also Lesson 21.)

Lesson 15

ASKING QUESTIONS

Dialogue 20

Amma: Kofi, wowɔ hɛ̃?	Kofi, where are you?
Kofi: Mewɔ dan mu.	I'm in the room.
Mewɔ pia mu [piem] ha.	I'm here in the bedroom.
Na ɛhɛ̃ na wo nso wowɔ?	And where are you too?
Amma: Mewɔ asaso.	I'm in the living room.
Adɛn, wohĩã me anaa?	Why, do you need me?
Kofi: Aane, bɛhwɛ adeɛ.	Yes, come and see something.
Wei yɛ deɛn/ɛdeɛn ni?	What is this?
Amma: ɛyɛ Abenaa nneɛma.	They are Abenaa's things.
Kofi: Da bɛn na ɔde baa ha?	When did she bring them here?
Amma: ɛbɛyɛ nna nan ni.	About (it will be) 4 days ago.
Kofi: ɛdeɛn na ɛwɔ mu?	What is inside it?
Amma: ɔse ɛyɛ kente ne batakari	She says they are kente and batakari (men's toga)
ne nneɛma nketenkete bi.	and some small items.
ɔde rekɔ [ɔdeekɔ] aburokyire.	She's taking them overseas.
Kofi: Da bɛn na ɔbɛkɔ aburokyire?	When (what day) will she go abroad?
Amma: Aa, mennim.	Well, I don't know.
Kofi: Adɛn, ɔankã [wankã] ankyerɛ wo?	Why, didn't she tell you?
Amma: Daabi.	No.
Kofi: Adɛn nti na woammisa [wæmmisa] no?	Why didn't you ask (why is it that you didn't ask) her?
Amma: Na ɔrepɛ ntɛm.	She was in a hurry.
ɔne obi na ɛbaeɛ.	She came with another person.
Kofi: Hwan na ɔne no baeɛ?	Whom did she come with?
Amma: Awuraa bi.	A certain lady.
Mennim no.	I don't know her.

Vocabulary

ɛhɛ̃?	where?	eg. ɛhɛ̃ na ɛwɔ/ Where is it?
		ɛwɔ hɛ̃?

66

εdeεn	what thing?		εdeεn ni?	What is this?
(from: adeε bεn)			Wopε deεn?	What do you want?
anaa	question word for		εyε anaa?:	Is it good?
	'yes-no' questions			
bεn	what?		Sika bεn?:	Which money?
bere bεn	when/what time?			
da bεn	when/what day?			
afe bεn	which year?			
adεn	why?			
adεn nti	why is it? (emphatic)			
pia	bedroom			
asaso	living room			
hĩă	to need / to be in need			
ohĩă	poverty			
ohĩăni	a poor person			
nneεma	things (plural of 'adeε' plus 'ma' dimunitive suffix)			
nketenkete	little (used with a plural noun; eg. mmofra nketenkete: several little children)			

Grammar points

Negative of the Past verb
    The Negative form of the Past verb has a prefix 'a-' in addition to the negative prefix 'm-' or 'n-', as in the following examples.

Positive		Negative	
Kofi kɔe	Kofi went.	Kofi ankɔ.	Kofi didn't go.
Wobisae.	You asked.	Woammisa.	You didn't ask.
ɔkă kyerεε me.	S/he told me.	ɔankă [wankă] ankyerε me.	
			S/he didn't tell me.

    Note that the last sentence contains the serial verb 'kă kyerε' (tell), from kă (say); kyerε (show/point out).

EXERCISE

Say the following in Twi:
    Where are they?   When (what time) did he go?
    How is Kofi?   When (what day) will he come?
    Who came here?   Why didn't Abenaa come?
    Why is s/he crying?   Did Afua go to the market?
    Where did you go?   Why didn't you eat the rice?
    What is this?   Is Kofi in New York / London?

Lesson 16

TELLING THE TIME

Dialogue 21

Mary: Kofi, maahã.	Kofi, good afternoon.
Kofi: Yaa nua. εte sεn?	(response) How is it?
Mary: εyε. Na wo nso ε?	Fine. And you?
Kofi: Me hõ yε.	I'm fine.
Mary, abɔ sεn?	Mary, what's the time?
	(It has struck how many times?)
Mary: Abɔ dɔn ko.	It is (has struck) one o'clock.
Kofi: Saa? Menim sε abɔ	Really? I thought (know) it is
dɔn ko ne fã.	half past one (1 hour and-a-half).
Mary: Daabi, aka simma aduasã.	No, there are 30 minutes more.
	(it is left 30 minutes)
Kofi: εnneε merekɔ sukuu.	Then I'm going to school.
Mεba fie nnɔn mmeεnsã.	I'll come home at 3 o'clock.
Mary: Me nso merekɔ laebri.	I'm also going to the library.
Mεba nnɔn nan apa hõ	I'll come home at 4.15pm.
simma dunum.	(4 o'clock has been gone 15
	minutes)
Kofi: Saa? Na bere bεn na	Is that so? And when will you
wobεkɔ wo maame hɔ?	go to your mother's place?
Mary: Mefi laebri ba a na mεkɔ.	When I come from the library,
	I'll go.
Kofi: εnneε twεn me. Mεba	O.K. then, wait for me. I'll come
na mene wo akɔ.	and go with you.
Mary: Yoo.Mεhwε w'anim.	OK. I'll expect you.

Vocabulary

dɔn	hour ('bell' - reference to the chiming of the clock)
nnɔn	hours
simma	minute(s)
bɔ	to strike / to ring a bell
	eg. abɔ dɔn ko : It is one o'clock (it has struck one bell).
(ε)fã	half
ka	to remain / to be left
pa hõ	go past / overtake

Grammar points

The Perfect verb

Note the use of the Perfect verb in telling the time:

Abɔ (dɔn ko).	It has struck (one o'clock).
Aka (simma aduasã).	It is left (30 minutes).
Nnɔn nan apa hɔ simma du.	It is ten past four. (4 o'clock has been gone for 10 mins.)

EXERCISE

Revise numbers (Lesson 5, Dialogue 5) and do the exercise below.

1. Tell the time in Twi. Here are a few examples:

It is 6.00 o'clock:	Abɔ nnɔn nsia.
6.10	Abɔ nnɔn nsia apa hɔ simma du.
6.40	Abɔ nnɔn nsia apa hɔ simma aduanan.
OR	Aka simma aduonu na abɔ nnɔn nson.
	(i.e. it is 20 minutes to 7 o'clock)

It is	10.00 o'clock	10.45
	11.30	9.20
	3.15	5.30
	2.10	8.00 o'clock

Time of day :

anɔpa	morning
anɔpa tutu / hema	early in the morning
awia	afternoon
anwumere	evening
anadwo	night

eg. 9.00 a.m.	anɔpa nnɔn nkron
6.00 p.m.	anwummere nnɔn nsĩã
1.20 p.m.	awia dɔn ko apa hɔ simma aduonu
9.45 p.m.	aka simma dunum na abɔ anadwo nnɔn du
	(15 minutes to 10 pm)

2. Express the following in Twi:

7.00 a.m.	9.40 a.m.
8.30 a.m.	3.20 p.m.
5.45 p.m.	12.00 noon
4.30 p.m.	12.00 midnight
10.10 p.m.	2.40 pm.

Dialogue 22

Amma: Abenaa, maakyě	Good morning, Abenaa.
Abenaa: Yaa asɔn. Ɛte sɛn?	(response) How is it?
Amma: Ɛyɛ. Wo nso ɛ?	Fine. And you?
Abenaa: Ɛyɛ.	Fine.
Amma: Worekɔ hě anɔpa tutu yi?	Where are you going this early morning?
Abenaa: Merekɔ adwuma.	I'm going to work.
Amma: Worekɔ adwuma ɛnnɛ Memeneda yi?	Are you going to work today, a Saturday?
Abenaa: Mankɔ adwuma nnaawɔtwe enti mewɔ adwuma pii yɛ.	I didn't go to work for a week so there's a lot of work that I have to do.
Amma: Adɛn, na woyare anaa?	Why, were you ill? (was it that you were ill?)
Abenaa: Daabi, metuu kwan. Mekɔɔ Nigeria. Mebaa nnansǎ ne nnɛ.	No, I travelled. I went to Nigeria. I came three days ago (3 days today).
Amma: Akwaaba. Ɛhɔ te sɛn?	Welcome. How is the place?
Abenaa: Ɛhɔ yɛ. Mɛkɔ hɔ bio akɔyɛ adwuma bi wɔ hɔ bosome a ɛreba [ɛɛba] yi.	It is fine. I'll go there again to do some work there next month (the month that is coming)
Amma: Saa? Wokɔ a nante yie.	Is that so? Have a good trip. (when you go walk well)
Abenaa: Oo, mɛhǔ wo ansǎ na makɔ.	Oh, I'll see you before I go.
Amma: Yoo, ɛnnɛɛ akyire yi yɛbɛhyia.	OK. See you later.
Abenaa: Yoo, baae.	OK. Goodbye.

Vocabulary

adwuma	work
ɛnnɛ	today
nnaawɔtwe	one week (8 days)
nnansǎ	three days
(nnansǎ yi	these days; in recent times)
bosome	month
abosome	months

70

Other expressions of time

ade akyɛ	it is morning
awia abɔ	the sun is up / it is afternoon
onwunu adwo	it is evening
ade asã	it is night / dark
ɛnnora	yesterday
ɔkyena	tomorrow
nnaawɔtwe a atwa mu yi	last week (the week that is past)
nnaawɔtwe a ɛreba yi	next week (the week that is coming)
bosome a ɛreba yi	next month
bosome a atwa mu yi	last month
afeda / afe a ɛreba yi	next year
afe a atwa mu yi	last year (the year that is past)
mfeɛ nan akyi	after four years

EXRECISE

Express the following in Twi:
   I saw him/her last week.
   I'll go to Togo next year.
   Why haven't you come here for a week?
   These days I don't see you at all.
   We'll see (meet) you tomorrow.
   They will go home next month.
   I'll come in the morning (when it is morning, I'll come).
   I feel hot, the sun is up.

71

Lesson 17

CULTURAL SITUATIONS

Dialogue 23 At a festival

Afua:	Amma yɛahyia [yæhyia].	Amma, well met (we've met).
Amma:	Yaa nua.	(response)
	Mpɔ mu [mpom] ɛ?	How are you (the joints)?
Afua:	ɛyɛ.	Fine.
	Na wo nso ɛ?	And you?
Amma:	Onyame adom ɛyɛ.	By God's grace, fine.
Afua:	ɛnnɛ afahyɛ yi bɛyɛ fɛ paa.	The festival today will be very beautiful.
	Hwɛ sɛnea	Look at how
	yɛasiesie ha afa.	they've decorated (here) this place.
Amma:	Mate sɛ Otumfoɔ	I've heard that Otumfoɔ
	ankasa bɛba bi.	(Asante King) himself will be coming too.
Afua:	Oo saa? Metee sɛ ɔbɛma	Oh really? I heard that he will
	ɔmanhene baakõ, ne kyɛãme	let one paramount chief, his
	ne ɔheneba abɛgyina	spokesman and his son
	[abegyina] n'anan mu.	represent him (stand in his stead).
	Yɛse ɔntumi [ontumi] mma.	They say he can't come.
Amma:	Wo deɛ no bɛyɛ nokorɛ.	Yours (your version) must be correct.
	Hwɛ odikro na ɔreba	Look, here comes the chief
	a twene di n'anim	(ruler of the town) preceded by the drums, and
	na kyiniɛ si ne so no.	with an umbrella over him.
	Ne hõ ayɛ fɛ paa.	He is looking very handsome.
	Ahennie no fata no paa.	The chiefly status really suits him.
Afua:	Woahũ ɔhemaa nso?	Have you seen the queenmother too?
	Ne hõ ayɛ fɛ papa.	She is looking very beautiful.
	Ma yɛmpɛ baabi papa	Let's look for a good place
	nnyina, na yɛahũ nea ɛrekɔ	to stand, so that we can see
	so no nyinaa.	everything that is going on.

Vocabulary

yεahyia	well met (a greeting used when people meet accidentally or at a function. Note the Perfect form of the verb: Yεahyia. We've met.)
afahyε	festival
sεnea	how (conjunction)
siesie	to decorate / to tidy up
Otumfoɔ	the powerful one, a title reserved for the Asantehene (King of the Asante)
ankasa	himself/herself/myself etc. (an emphatic particle)
ɔmanhene	paramount chief (see culture points below) (from: ɔman : state; ɔhene : chief)
ɔkyeame	the chief's spokesman (linguist)
ɔheneba	a chief's son/daughter
gyina anan mu	to represent /to stand in for (gyina: to stand; anan: legs; mu: inside)
odikro	chief (di: rule; kuro: town / village)
twene	drum(s)
kyiniε	umbrella (one of the symbols of chieftaincy is a big colourful umbrella that somebody holds over the head of the chief on formal occasions)
ahennie	chiefly status (from: di (ɔ)hene : become chief)
ɔhemaa	'queenmother'; she may be the mother, sister or the maternal aunt or cousin of the chief. She sits in state next to the chief at a function. She may also be a chief, the sole ruler of a town. (ɔhene: chief; (ɔ)baa: woman)
pε	look for / search
kɔ so	go on; continue
nyinaa	all; everything

Culture points

1. Chieftaincy in the Asante kingdom has a hierarchical structure headed by the Asantehene. He is the occupant of the Golden Stool, which symbolises the 'soul' of the Asante people. It is the one symbol that unifies the Asante, and helped to make them a powerful nation.
   Below the Asantehene are a number of chiefs (amanhene) who have jurisdiction over a number of towns and villages that constitute a unit or a state within the Asante kingdom.
   Below the ɔmanhene, every town or village has a chief (ɔhene / odikro) whose jurisdiction is limited to the particular town or village over which he rules.

2. Asantes are matrilineal, that is, they trace their lineage through the mother. The chief's children cannot therefore inherit their father, and are not part of the 'royal' family, whose members are referred to as 'adehyeɛ'. A chief's child can only be referred to as 'ɔheneba' (ɔhene: chief; ɔba: child). The term 'prince' or 'princess' is not quite appropriate, since an ɔheneba cannot inherit the father's position and title the way a prince or princess can.
3. The Asante calendar is reckoned in a forty-day cycle, and the final Sunday of this cycle is celebrated as the Akwasidae or Adae festival, when the chief sits in state and receives homage from his subjects.

EXERCISE

Describe a festival or any ceremonial occasion that you have seen.

Dialogue 24   Naming ceremony

Kofi:	Abenaa yɛahyia.	Abenaa, well met.
Abenaa:	Yaa nua.	(response)
Kofi:	Worekɔ hɛ na woayɛ fitaa yi?	Where are you going and you are in (you've done) white?
Abenaa:	Me nua Kwame reto [ɛɛto] ne ba din, ɛna merekɔboa no.	My brother, Kwame, is naming his child, and I'm going to help him.
Kofi:	Ei, saa? Ne yere woo da bɛn?	Really? When did his wife have a baby?
Abenaa:	ɛnnɛ ne nnaawɔtwe.	A week today (today is a week).
Kofi:	ɔwoo deɛn?	What (boy or girl) did she give birth to?
Abenaa:	ɔwoo ɔbaa. Kwame se ɔde no bɛto yɛn maame, enti yɛbɛfrɛ no Sɛɛwaa	She had a girl. Kwame says he will name her after our mother and so she will be called Sɛɛwaa.
Kofi:	Ka kyerɛ Kwame ne ne yere sɛ mema wɔn tiri nkwa. Ka kyerɛ akɔdaa no nso sɛ mema no aba a tena ase.	Tell Kwame and his wife that I congratulate them. Tell the baby too that I wish her long life (if she has come, she should {sit down} stay).
Abenaa:	Yoo, wɔɔnom bɛte.	OK. I'll tell them (they'll hear).

Vocabulary

fitaa	white
to din	to give a name to / to name
boa	to help
mmoa	help (n)
wo	to give birth
awoɔ	chilbearing
akɔdaa	child; infant
tena ase	sit down

Culture points

1. White is the colour worn on happy occasions, such as on the birth of a child, at a wedding or a marriage ceremony, on winning a court case and so on.
2. Every Akan child is formally given a name on the eighth day after its birth, (which will be the same day of the week as the day on which s/he was born) or soon after that day if for some reason, such as the mother or the baby being unwell, this cannot be done on the eighth day.
3. It is the father who has the right to give the child a name, and he normally will name him/her after his parent or a member of his family, dead or alive, whose character he would like the child to emulate. Many such names have male and female versions. (See Appendix II for more information on Akan names.)
4. 'Aba a tena ase' : (from: woaba a tena ase) 'now that you have come, do stay'. This is a greeting that is said to an infant to wish the child long life. It is also said to a new wife by her in-laws to wish her a long successful marriage.

Dialogue 25   Marriage

Afua:	Amma yɛahyia.	Amma, well met.
Amma:	Yaa nua.	(response)
	Mpɔ mu ɛ?	How are you?
Afua:	ɛyɛ. Na wo nso ɛ?	Fine. And you?
Amma:	ɛyɛ. Worekɔ hɛ	Fine. Where are you going
	na wo hő ayɛ fɛ sei?	that you look so beautiful?
Afua:	Yɛkɔgyee yere maa me	We went and married (received)
	wɔfa.	a wife for my uncle.
Amma:	Yɛda Onyame ase.	We thank God.

75

	ɔbaa hwan na ɔwaree no?	Which woman did he marry?
Afua:	Maame Akosua ba Nana Yaa.	Maame Akosua's daughter Nana Yaa.
Amma:	Lɔya no?	The lawyer?
Afua:	Aane.	Yes.
Amma:	ɛnneɛ moakɔbɔ ka.	Then you must have spent a lot of money (you've incurred debt).
Afua:	Oo, yɛammɔ ka kɛse pii. N'awofoɔ se me wɔfa bɛhyia no ayeforɔ enti ɛka pii da yɛanim.	Oh, we didn't spend a lot of money. Her parents say my uncle will wed her, and so we will be spending a lot of money (there is a lot of debt in front of us).
	Wɔɔnom gyee ne ti nsã ne ne maame ne papa deɛ ketewa bi.	They took (from us) the 'head drink' and a small something for her mother and her father.
Amma:	Na ɔbaa no momaa no deɛn?	And the woman, what did you give her?
Afua:	Yɛde adaka a ne ntoma ne nneɛma kakra wɔ mu,	We gave her a suitcase (box) in which her cloth and a few other things were packed,
	ɛne ne sika a ɛda so maa no.	and we added her money (put it on top).
Amma:	Na wo wɔfa nkonta nso ɛ?	How about your uncle's brothers-in-law?
Afua:	Ei, wɔɔnom haa yɛn paa. Yɛse yɛmma me wɔfa mfa wɔɔnom nuabaa no nkɔ.	They really gave us a tough time. They said they would not allow my uncle to take their sister away.
	Yɛpaa kyɛw kyɛree ansã na wɔɔnom repene [ɛɛpene].	We pleaded (with them) for a long time before they agreed.
Amma:	ɛnneɛ moakɔyɛ adwuma nnɛ.	Well, you have done (a lot of) work today.
Afua:	Aane, ɛsɛ w'ani.	Yes, you should have seen it.
	ɛyɛɛ fɛ paa.	It was really nice.
Amma:	Mo ne adwuma.	Congratulations on a (good) job done.
Afua:	Yaa nua.	(response)

Vocabulary

gye yere	to marry; take a wife for another person
bɔ ka	to incur debt; spend a lot of money

76

awofoɔ	parents (wo: to give birth)
hyia ayeforɔ	to have a western-style wedding ceremony
hyia	to meet
ayeforɔ	bride (yere: wife; (fo)forɔ: new)
ɛka	debt; a lot of expenditure
ti nsá	drink that is given to a woman's family to signify that a marriage has taken place. It is usually shared among members of the family to indicate that they are all witnesses to the marriage
adaka	box; in this context a suitcase or a trunk for keeping clothes in
akonta	brother-in-law
nkontanom	(plural)
ha	to bother; give trouble
de/fa kä	to add
pene	agree
adwuma	work

Culture points

1. Marriage is a union between the families of both the man and the woman, and so whatever age the two people are, a man and a woman cannot just decide to walk into a marriage registrar's office and get married. The man's parents or head of family sends a delegation to inform the woman's parents or head of family of their intention to marry the woman for their son. On the appointed day, the man's relations and the woman's relations hold a formal gathering. The man's relations present drinks 'ti nsá' and some money to the woman's parents and the head of family; they also present gifts in the form of clothing, jewellery and money to the wife, and give money to the woman's brothers and maternal male cousins to allow the husband to take the woman away. The brothers-in-law are expected to refuse what is offered the first time, and a lot of negotiation goes on till a final sum is agreed on. There is a lot of play-acting that takes place during marriage ceremonies, since whatever the man's relations bring would have been discussed with and agreed upon by the woman and her parents before the day of the marriage ceremony. The acceptance and drinking of the 'ti nsá' is what signifies that a marriage contract has been entered into.

2. After this traditional marriage ceremony, the couple may decide to register their marriage as a customary marriage (which is potentially polygamous) or they may decide to have

a western-style wedding (which is monogamous). In this case the traditional marriage is considered by many as an engagement.

Dialogue 26   Funeral

Mary:	Abenaa, maahã	Good afternoon, Abenaa.
Abenaa:	Yaa asɔn.	(response)
	Adɛn, tuntum yi ɛ?	Why are you in black (this black)?
Mary:	Hm, m'adamfo bi na ɔaka [waka] baabi [bææbi].	Hm, it is a friend of mine who is dead (has been left behind somewhere).
Abenaa:	Oo, kosɛ / due.	Oh, my sympathies.
	Owuu da bɛn?	When did she die?
Mary:	Nnawɔtwe mmienu ne nnɛ.	It is two weeks today.
	ɔkyena na yɛbɛsie no.	It is tomorrow that we will bury her.
Abenaa:	Mobɛyɛ ayie no abɔ mu [abom]?	Will you perform (do) the funeral rites together (i.e. immediately after the burial)?
Mary:	Aane.	Yes.
Abenaa:	Sɛ woka kyerɛɛ me a ankã mɛkɔ akɔgya [akogya] wo.	If you had told me, I would have gone with you (to give you support).
	Meretu [miitu] kwan ɔkyena.	I'm travelling tomorrow.
Mary:	M'adwene nyinaa ayɛ basaa	My mind is all confused (by the shock of the death)
	enti fa kyɛ me.	so forgive me.
	Ma yɛnkɔ na kɔkyea kunafoɔ no ɛ?	Shall we go and greet the widower?
Abenaa:	Oo, me ntoma yi nyɛ.	Oh, my cloth is not good.
Mary:	Adɛn, ɛte sɛn?	Why, what's wrong with it?
	ɛyɛ.	It is OK.
	ɛnyɛ fitaa yi deɛ, ɛyɛ.	Once it is not white, it is OK
	Mɛdi w'anim na yɛakɔkyea.	I will lead you to go and greet (him).
Abenaa:	Yoo, di kan na menni w'akyi.	OK. You lead and I'll follow (behind).

78

Vocabulary

ka baabi	euphemism for 'to die' (wu)
	(ka : to be left behind; baabi : somewhere)
wu	to die
ayie	rites performed after the burial
bɔ mu	to combine, to do together
ankä	conjunction after an 'if' clause

eg. (Sɛ) mehũũ kwadu no a ankä mɛtɔ bi.

If I had seen the bananas, I would have bought some.

kɔgya [kogya]	to go with; accompany
adwene	mind; brain
basaa	confused; messy
fa kyɛ	to forgive (take give)
kunafoɔ	widow / widower
di kan	to lead; go in front / ahead
di akyi	to follow

Culture points

1. Very dark colours are used for funerals; black is especially used if the deceased is a close friend or a relation.
2. After burial, the family and all sympathisers gather at the house of the deceased or at a central place for what is called 'ayie', the final funeral rites. This consists in the sympathisers being offered drinks, after which they give donations of money to help the bereaved family defray some of the cost of the funeral. The burial and the 'ayie' may take place the same day, especially if the dead body was kept in the mortuary long enough for the family to make the necessary arrangements for the 'ayie'. Otherwise, the body may be buried soon after the death has occurred, and the 'ayie' is organised at a later date.
3. People are expected to go and sympathise with the bereaved family, even when they are not close friends or related to them, so Abenaa agrees to go with Mary to 'greet' the widower.

PART II

Understanding the Grammar

INTRODUCTION

Aspects of the grammar of Twi were discussed as they came up in the lessons in Part I. Part II now deals with the grammar of the language in a more systematic manner. These are also illustrated with dialogues where necessary.

It was pointed out in Part I that verbs occur with a number of affixes which are used to indicate tense and aspect. It was also noted that verbal affixes have two pronunciations depending on the vowel of the verb stem. Affixes occuring with nouns also have two pronunciations depending on the vowel of the nominal stem, so that Twi vowels generally fall into two groups, with vowels of only one group normally occurring in any given word. This is a common feature of the Akan language as a whole, and is referred to as vowel harmony. The following examples illustrate this point. The stems are italicized in each case.

	Group 1 e ɛ ɔ o a		Group 2 i e o u æ	
Verbs				
	ɔbɛ*da*	S/he will sleep.	Obe*di*	S/he will eat it.
	ɔ*kŏĕ*	S/he fought.	Ohŭ*ĭ*	S/he saw it.
	Yɛ*kasa*	We talk.	Ye*bisa*	We ask.
	Me*kŏ*	I fight.	Mi*hŭ*	I see it.
	Wo*tɔ*	You buy it.	Wu*di*	You eat it.
	Ma*gye*	I've received it.	Mæ*di*	I've eaten it.
Nouns				
	ɛbo*ɔ*	stone/price	ebu*o*	respect/bird's nest
	ase*ɛ*	bottm/base	esi*e*	anthill
	ɔ*hene*	chief	oni*ni*	python
	awo*ɔ*	childbearing	owu*o*	death

Note that e and o have two pronunciations each :

Group 1: e is pronounced as in *sit*
           o is pronounced as in *book*
Group 2 : e is pronounced as in *day*
           o is pronounced as in *go*

Lesson 18

HABITUAL, PROGRESSIVE, SIMPLE FUTURE

Habitual : The Habitual has no overt affix. The verb stem is usually said on a high tone, while the subject pronouns are normally said on low tone, except the 2nd person singular and plural subject prefixes which are said on high tone.

Mèdá	I sleep.	Kofi dá.	Kofi sleeps.
Wódá	You (sing.) sleep.	Amma kɔ́.	Amma goes.
ɔ̀dá	S/he sleeps.	Kofi dí.	Kofi eats.
Yɛ̀dá	We sleep.	Yaw ne Afua kɔ́.	Yaw and Afua go.
Módá	You (plu.) sleep.		
Wɔ́nɔ̌m dá/	They sleep.		
Yɛ̀dá			

Progressive : Prefix re- pronounced as a long vowel.

Merekɔ [meekɔ].	I'm going.	Meredi [miidi].	I'm eating it.
Worekɔ [wookɔ].	You're going.	Woredi [wuudi].	You're eating it.
ɔrekɔ [ɔɔkɔ].	S/he's going.	ɔredi [oodi].	S/he's eating it.
Yɛrekɔ [yɛɛkɔ].	We're going.	Yɛredi [yeedi].	We're eating it.
Kofi rekɔ.	Kofi is going.	Kofi redi.	Kofi is eating it.
[kofiikɔ]		[kofiidi]	

Future : Prefix bɛ- pronounced be- or bɛ- depending on the vowel of the verb. The full form of the prefix is not used in the first person singular.

Mɛda.	I will sleep.	Mɛhû [mehû].	We will see it.
Wobɛkɔ.	You will go.	Wobɛdi [wubedi].	You will eat it.
ɔbɛkɔ.	S/he will go.	Wɔɔnom bɛhû [behû].	They'll see it.
Kofi bɛda.	Kofi will sleep.	Afua bɛdi [bedi].	Afua will eat it.

Dialogue 27

Kofi:	Amma, maakyɛ̂	Good morning, Amma.	
Amma:	Yaa nua. ɛte sɛn?	(response) How is it?	
Kofi:	ɛyɛ. Wo nso ɛ?	Fine. And you?	

85

Kofi:	ɛyɛ. Wo nso ɛ?	Fine. And you?
Amma:	Me hɔ yɛ.	I'm fine.
	Kofi, worekɔ [wookɔ] hɛ̃?	Kofi, where are you going?
Kofi:	Merekɔ Kumase.	I'm going to Kumasi.
	Merekɔsra me maame.	I'm going to visit my mother.
Amma:	Wo maame te Kumase?	Does your mother live in Kumasi?
Kofi:	Aane, ɔte Kumase.	Yes, she lives in Kumasi.
Amma:	ɔfi [ofi] Kumase?	Is she from Kumasi?
Kofi:	Daabi [dææbi], ɔyɛ adwuma wɔ hɔ.	No, she works there.
Amma:	Wobɛdu [wubedu] Bɛkwae?	Will you get to (as far as) Bɛkwae?
Kofi:	Daabi, merekɔ Kumase nkōáá.	No, I'm going to Kumasi only.
Amma:	Wobɛba da bɛn?	When will you come back?
Kofi:	Mɛba ɔkyena.	I'll be back tomorrow.
Amma:	Yoo, nante yie.	All right, Goodbye (Have a good trip).
Kofi:	Yoo.	All right.

EXERCISE:

1. Read through the dialogue again. List the verbs that are in the: i) Habitual; ii) Progressive; iii) Future

2. Put the following verbs in the i) Habitual
                                                      ii) Progressive
                                                      iii) Future
in the 1st., 2nd. and 3rd. person singular forms to complete the sentences below:
a) hwɛ (look at)   d) tɔ (buy)
b) bisa (ask)   Kofi   e) di (eat)   paanoo (bread)
c) frɛ (call)   f) tõ (bake)

Lesson 19

SIMPLE FUTURE, IMMEDIATE FUTURE

Simple Future : The Simple (indefinite) Future has the Prefix bɛ-

Immediate Future : The Immediate Future has the Prefix rebɛ-

Simple Future		Immediate Future	
Mɛkɔ.	I'll go.	Merebɛkɔ [meebɛkɔ].	I'm about to go.
Wobɛkɔ.	You'll go.	Worebɛkɔ [woobɛkɔ].	You're about to go.
ɔbɛkɔ.	S/he'll go.	ɔrebɛkɔ [ɔɔbɛkɔ].	S/he's about to go.
Yɛbɛkɔ.	We'll go.	Yɛrebɛkɔ [yɛɛbɛkɔ].	We're about to go.
Mobɛkɔ.	You'll go.	Morebɛkɔ [moobɛkɔ].	You're about to go.
Wɔɔnom bɛkɔ.	They'll go	Wɔɔnom rebɛkɔ [wɔɔnomoobɛkɔ].	They're about to go.
Yɛbɛkɔ.	They'll go	Yɛrebɛkɔ [yɛɛbɛkɔ].	They're about to go.

The rules of vowel harmony also apply as illustrated by the following examples:

Mɛdi [medi].
I'll eat it.

Merebɛdi [miibedi].
I'm about to eat it.

Wobɛdi [wubedi].
You'll eat it.

Worebɛdi [wuubedi].
You're about to eat it.

ɔbɛdi [obedi].
S/he'll eat it.

ɔrebɛdi [oobedi].
S/he's about to eat it.

Yɛbɛdi [yebedi].
We'll eat it.

Yɛrebɛdi [yeebedi].
We're about to eat it.

Mobɛdi [mubedi].
You'll eat it.

Morebɛdi [muubedi].
You're about to eat it.

The difference in meaning between the two forms of the verb is further illustrated by the following sentences.

Kofi bɛtɔ kaa afe yi.	Kofi will buy a car this year.
Kofi rebɛtɔ loto tikit.	Kofi is about to buy a lottery ticket.
ɔbɛyɛ, na ne ntɛm.	S/he will do it, but how quickly (soon).
ɔrebɛyɛ no seesei ara.	S/he's going to (about to) do it right now.
Mɛkɔ Nkran awia yi.	I will go to Accra this afternoon.
Merebɛkɔ Nkran seesei ara.	I'm about to go to Accra right now.

Dialogue 28

Mary: Amma wobɛkɔ sukuu ɛnnɛ?	Amma will you go to school today?
Amma: Aane. Merebɛdidi.	Yes. I'm going to eat.
Medidi wie a, mɛkɔ.	When I finish eating, I'll go.
Mary: ɛnneɛ mɛtwɛn wo.	Then I'll wait for you.
Amma: Merebɛnom tii.	I'm going to have (drink) tea.
Mewie a mɛto	When I finish, I'll iron
m'ataadeɛ.	my dress.
Wobɛkyɛ.	You will delay (keep long).
Kɔ na mɛba.	Go, (and) I'll come.
Mary: Yoo. Meredi kan.	All right. I'm taking the lead.

The following verbs occur in the dialogue. Check up their meanings and note the contexts in which they are used.

Simple Future: wobɛkɔ; mɛkɔ; mɛtwɛn; mɛto; wobɛkyɛ; mɛba
Immediate Future: merebɛdidi; merebɛnom
Progressive: meredi (kan)
Habitual: mewie

Note : di (to eat) is a transitive verb, and is used with an object. Where the object is not overtly expressed, it is the non-animate object 'it'.
The reduplicated form, didi, is an intransitive verb.

eg. ɔdi [odi] fufuo. S/he eats fufu.   ɔdi [odi]. S/he eats it.

ɔdidi [odidi].   S/he eats. (eg. often/a lot/sometimes)

EXERCISE

Put the following verbs in the
               i) Simple Future
               ii) Immediate Future
of the 1st., 2nd. and 3rd. person plural to complete the sentences below.

a) hʊ (see/consult)   d) di (eat)
b) frɛ (call)   Kofi   e) noa (cook)   ɛmo (rice)
c) boa (help)   f) tɔn (sell)

Lesson 20

THE NEGATIVE OF
THE HABITUAL, PROGRESSIVE, SIMPLE
FUTURE AND IMMEDIATE FUTURE

POSITIVE	NEGATIVE

POSITIVE

Kofi kɔ hɔ. (Hab.)
Kofi goes there.

Kofi rekɔ hɔ. (Pro.)
Kofi is going there.

Kofi bɛkɔ hɔ. (S.Fut.)
Kofi will go there.

Kofi rebɛkɔ hɔ. (Im.Fut.)
Kofi is about to go there.

NEGATIVE

Kòfí ǹkɔ̀ hɔ́

Kofi doesn't go there.

Kofi isn't going there.

Kofi won't go there.

Kofi isn't about to go there.

The above sentences show how one negative form negates all the four affirmative sentences. In other words, the differences in the forms of the Habitual, the Progressive, the Simple and Immediate Future are not maintained in the negative forms of the verb. Here is another example:

POSITIVE

Amma pam ataadeɛ.
Amma sews a dress.

Amma repam ataadeɛ.
Amma is sewing a dress.

Amma bɛpam ataadeɛ.
Amma will sew a dress.

Amma rebɛpam ataadeɛ.
Amma is about to sew a dress.

NEGATIVE

Amma m̀pám àtàadéɛ.

Amma doesn't sew a dress.

Amma isn't sewing a dress.

Amma won't sew a dress.

Amma isn't about to sew a dress.

However, when the verb has a pronoun subject, there is a difference in the tonal pattern of the Habitual Negative on the one hand, and the negative of the Progressive, Simple and Immediate Future on the other.

POSITIVE   NEGATIVE

ɔkɔ. (Hab)   S/he goes.   ɔ̀ǹkɔ́   S/he doesn't go.

ɔrekɔ. (Pro)   S/he's going.   S/he's not going.

ɔbɛkɔ. (S.Fut)   S/he will go.   ɔ́ǹkɔ́   S/he won't go.

ɔrebɛkɔ. (Im.Fut) S/he's about to go.   S/he isn't about to go.

| Yɛkasa. (Hab) | We talk. | yɛ̀ǹkàsá | We don't talk. |

Yɛrekasa. (Pro)	We're talking.		We're not talking.
Yɛbɛkasa. (S.Fut)	We will talk.	yɛ̀ǹkàsá	We won't talk.
Yɛrebɛkasa. (Im.Fut)			We're not about to
	We're about to talk.		talk.

EXERCISE:

Put the verbs below in the Negative of the Habitual, Progressive, Simple Future and the Immediate Future, and complete the sentences.

		a) tɔn	(sell)	
Kofi / I / we		b) di	(eat)	kwadu (bananas)
		c) tɔ	(buy)	

Lesson 21

PAST, PERFECT

Past : The past form of the verb is indicated by the Suffix -e /-i: -e for verbs with Group 1 vowels, and -i for verbs with Group 2 vowels, according to the rules of vowel harmony, as in:

Kofi kɔe̱.	Kofi fought.	Kofi hṳ̀i̱.	Kofi saw it.
Afua tɔe.	Afua bought it.	Afua dii.	Afua ate it.

There are two forms of the Past verb:

i) When there is no complement, the suffix -e/-i occurs after the verb:

Mekɔe.	I went.
ɔpamee.	S/he sewed it.
Yɛhṳ̀i̱ [yehṳ̀i̱].	We saw it. (non-animate)
ɛdumii [edumii].	It (light/fire) went out.

ii) When there is a complement, the suffix is realised as a lengthening of the final vowel or consonant of the verb:

Mekɔɔ hɔ.	I went there.
ɔpamm ataadeɛ.	S/he sewed a dress.
Yɛhṳ̀ṳ̀ [yehṳ̀ṳ̀] no.	We saw him.
ɔdumm gya no.	S/he put out the fire.

Perfect : The Perfect aspect is indicated by the Prefix a-

Mafa	I've taken it	Mafa sika.	I've taken money.
ɔapam [wapam].	S/he's sewn it.	ɔapam ataadeɛ.	S/he's sewn a dress.
Yɛatɔn [yatɔn].	We've sold it.	Yɛatɔn ataadeɛ.	We've sold a dress.
Yɛadi [yædi].	We've eaten it.	Yɛadi ɛmo.	We've eaten rice.

Dialogue 29

Kofi: Yaw, wokɔɔ Kumase no bi?	Yaw, did you go to Kumasi too?
Yaw: Aane, mekɔe.	Yes, I went.
Me ne Kwame na yɛkɔeɛ.	I and Kwame went.
Kofi: Wohṳ̀ṳ̀ [wuhṳ̀ṳ̀] Kwasi?	Did you see Kwasi?
Yaw: Aane, ɔayɛ [wayɛ] kɛse paa.	Yes. He has put on weight. (He has become very big.)

91

Kofi: Yɛama [yama] no kaa ne draeva, enti ɛhɔ yɛ ma no.

They've given him a car and a driver, so the place is good for him.

Yaw: Aane, ɔhwɛɛ yɛn yiye paa.

Yes, he took very good care of us.

Kofi: ɛnneɛ moakɔgye mo ani wɔ Kumase. Akwaaba.

Well, you have gone and enjoyed yourselves in Kumasi. Welcome (back).

The following are the Past and Perfect verbs in the dialogue. Check up their meanings and note the contexts in which they are used.

Past: wokɔɔ, wohũũ, ɔhwɛɛ (with complement)
         mekɔe, yɛkɔeɛ (without complement)

Perfect: ɔayɛ, yɛama, moakɔgye.

Note additional Grammar points
1. yɛkɔeɛ : this Past form with an additional -ɛ suffix occurs after the emphatic particle 'na', as in : Me ne Kwame na yɛkɔeɛ. (It is Kwame and I who went.)

2. yɛama no: they have given him ...(he's been given..)
         Twi expresses what translates as the Passive in English with the 3rd. person plural. (Note that Asante speakers use yɛ   for both 1st. and 3rd. person plural.)

eg. kosua a yɛanoa   boiled egg (egg that they have boiled)
    Yɛawia no.   S/he's been robbed (they've robbed him).
    Yɛasoma no.   S/he's been sent on an errand (they've sent him/her).

EXERCISE:

Complete the following sentences by giving the 1st., 2nd.anc 3rd. person singular forms of the verbs in the
    i) Past - with a complement
          - without a complement
    ii) Perfect

a) hũ (see / consult)   d) tɔ (bake)
b) hwehwɛ (look for) Afua   e) di (eat)   paanoo (bread)
c) frɛ (call)   f) tɔn (sell)

92

Lesson   22

THE NEGATIVE OF THE PAST AND PERFECT

The affixes of the Past and Perfect forms of the verb switch over between the positive and negative forms of the verb.

Negative Past: Prefix a- plus the negative prefix
Negative Perfect: Suffix -e / -i plus the negative prefix

Past:

	POSITIVE		NEGATIVE	
ɔfae.	S/he took it.	ɔamfa [wamfa].	S/he didn't take it.
ɔkɔɔ hɔ.	S/he went there.	ɔankɔ [wankɔ] hɔ.	S/he didn't go there.
Mepamee.	I sewed it.	Mampam.	I didn't sew it.
Yɛhûû no.	We saw him.	Yɛanhû [yænhû] no.	We didn't see him.

Perfect:

	POSITIVE		NEGATIVE	
ɔafa [wafa].	S/he's taken it.	ɔmfae.	S/he hasn't taken it.
ɔaba [waba] ha.	S/he's been here.	ɔmmaa ha.	S/he hasn't been here.
Matɔn.	I've sold it.	Mentɔnee.	I haven't sold it.
Yɛahû [yæhû].	We've seen it.	Yɛnhûî.	We haven't seen it.

EXERCISE

Complete the sentences below by giving the Negative forms of the 1st., 2nd. and 3rd. person singular of the following verbs in the
  i) Past - with a complement
         - without a complement
  ii) Perfect

  a) hû (see / consult)
  b) hwehwɛ (look for)   Afua
  c) frɛ (call)
  d) tõ (bake)
  e) di (eat)   paanoo (bread)
  f) tɔn (sell)

Lesson 23

SIMPLE AND OPTATIVE IMPERATIVE

Simple Imperative: the simple verb, no affixes

eg. kɔ   go!   fa   take it!   bra   come!
     bisa   ask!   yɛ/yɔ   do it!   bu   break it!

Optative Imperative : Prefix m-/n- plus an optional low tone 'mà' (let). It occurs with all the subject pronouns except the second person singular. The whole verb is said on high pitch.

eg. Mà ɔ́ńkɔ́.   Let him/her go.   Mà ɔ́ḿfá.   Let him/her take it.
    Ɔ́ńkɔ.   Let him/her go.   Ɔ́ḿfá   Let him/her take it.
    Yɛ́ńkɔ́.   Let's go.   Yɛ́ḿfá.   Let's take it.
    Mɔ́ńhwɛ́.   You (plu.) look at it.   Mɔ́ńnidi′   You (plu) eat !
                                             [munnidi].
    Ma Kofi ntɔ kawa no.   Let Kofi buy the ring.
    Momfa mmienu nkɔ.   Take two away (take two and go).
    Ma memfa nkɔ.   Let me take it away.
    Ma wɔɔnom ntɔn.   Let them sell it.

This form of the verb is used for asking permission to do something:
   Menkɔ?   May I go?   Yɛmmra mu?   May we come in?
   ɔmmfa?   Should s/he take it?   Menkɔtɔ?   May I go and buy it?

Negative of the Simple and Optative Imperative

Negative prefix : m-/ n-
Simple Imperative

POSITIVE		NEGATIVE	
kɔ	go!	nkɔ	don't go!
di·	eat it!	nni	don't eat it!
pam	sew it!	mpam	don't sew it!
tɔn	sell it!	ntɔn	don't sell it!
bra	come!	mma	don't come!

(*Note:* the verb 'bra' (come) is the only verb that has two forms: 'bra' for the Positive Imperative, both Simple and Optative, and 'ba' for all other forms of the verb.)

Optative Imperative

POSITIVE		NEGATIVE	
Mà ɔ́ńkɔ́.	Let him go.	m̀má ɔ̀ǹnkɔ́.	Don't let him go.
Mà Kòfi'ńtɔ́.	Let Kofi buy it.	m̀má Kòfi'ǹtɔ́.	Don't let Kofi buy it.
Ma ɔmmfa.	Let him take it.	Mma ɔmmfa.	Don't let him take it.
Monhwehwɛ.	Look for it.	Monnhwehwɛ.	Don't look for it.
Ma ɔmmra.	Let him come.	Mma ɔmmma.	Don't let him come.

The difference between the Positive and Negative forms of the Optative Imperative is in tone, as shown in the first two examples, and not in the length of the m-/n- prefix. In other words, the mm-/nn- of the Negative is pronounced as a single m-/n-. The prefix is on high tone in the Positive and on low tone in the Negative.

EXERCISE

Select any five verbs you know and put them in
    a) Positive
    b) Negative
forms of the Simple and Optative Imperative.

Lesson 24

CONSECUTIVE

The Consecutive form of the verb is indicated by the Prefix a- .
This form of the verb occurs in serial verb sentences after the
Progressive and Future forms of the verb. It usually has a future
meaning, for example:

Kofi rekɔ akɔfa adaka no aba.	Kofi is going to bring (will take, will come) the box.
Kofi bɛkɔ akɔfa adaka no aba.	Kofi will go and bring the box.
Kofi rebɛkɔ akɔfa adaka no aba.	Kofi is about to go and bring the box.
ɔbɛtɔ nwoma no akan.	S/he will buy the book and read it.
Merebɛtena ha adidi.	I'm going to sit here and eat.
Mɛtɔ aduane adi.	I'll buy food and eat it.
ɔhene no bɛgyina ha akasa.	The chief will stand here to speak.
Wobɛtɔn ataadeɛ no agye sika?	Will you sell the dress for (receive) money?

The Consecutive verbs are: akɔfa, aba, akan, adidi, adi,
akasa, agye.
Note the contexts in which they are used.

EXERCISE

Express the following sentences in Twi. The verbs you need are
indicated for each sentence.

I'll buy bread and eat it.	(tɔ, di)
Kofi is about to go and sell the book.	(kɔ, tɔn)
I'm going to take the dress and come.	(fa, ba)
Amma will cook food (aduane) and eat it.	(noa, di)
I'm taking it for (give) him.	(fa, ma)

Negative Consecutive :	Same as the Progressive and Future Negative.
eg. Kofi nkɔ nkɔfa adaka no mma.	i) Kofi isn't going to bring the box.
	ii) Kofi won't go and bring the box.
	iii) Kofi isn't about to go and bring the box.

96

The following are the negative of some of the remaining Twi sentences:

ɔntɔ nwoma no nkan.	S/he won't buy the book and read it.
Mentena ha nnidi.	I'm not going to sit here and eat.

EXERCISE

Give the Negative forms of the rest of
   a) The Twi sentences above;
   b) The English sentences in the exercise.

Lesson 25

STATIVE

The Stative form has no affix. It is not a frequently used form of the verb, and very few verbs occur in it. It is included here to give a complete picture of the different Tense and Aspect forms of the Twi verb. It is the same form as the Habitual, except that the Stative verb is said on low tone.

Habitual		Stative	
Kòfí´hyέ ! kyέ.	Kofi wears a hat.	Kòfí´hyὲ kyέ.	Kofi has a hat on.
Ɔ̀gy`iná há. [ogyina]	S/he stops here.	Ɔ̀gy`inὰ há.	S/he is standing here (and has been standing for some time).
Mɛ̀dá ! há.	I sleep here.	Mɛ̀dὰ há.	I'm lying down here (and have been so for some time).

Note: The exclamation mark ! in the Habitual sentences indicates that the high tone on 'kyε' or 'ha' is not as high as the one on the preceding syllable. See section on tone in Lesson 1.

The following verbs occur in the Stative only:

de	to be named / called / carry a name
de	to take
nim	to know
nyem	to be pregnant
te	to live in a place
sɔ̃	to be big
sɔ̃	to be carrying a load
sua [swa]	to be small
wɔ	to have

There are other verbs with the same meanings which replace these verbs in the other Tense/Aspect forms of the verb.

de	: frε	de	: fa (to take)
nim	: hũ	nyem	: nyinsεn
te	: tena	sɔ̃	: yε kεse (be big)
sɔ̃	: soa (to carry)	wɔ	: nya
sua	: yε ketewa (be small)		

eg. ɔde ba.   S/he brings it.   ɔmfa mma. S/he doesn't bring it.

98

Minim no. I know him/her.   Mɛhû no. I'll recognise him/her.
ɔsô.   S/he's big.   ɔayɛ kɛse. S/he has grown big.

The Negative of the Stative is sometimes the same as the
Habitual for some verbs, and different for others.

Habitual

ɔñhyɛ́ ! kyɛ́. S/he doesn't
wear a hat.

ɔñnyïná hɔ́. S/he doesn't
stop there.

Stative

ɔñhyɛ́ ! kyɛ́. S/he doesn't have
a hat on.

ɔñnyïná ! hɔ́. S/he's not standing
there.

EXERCISE

1. Practice the Habitual and Stative sentences above.
2. Express the following sentences in Twi, use the Stative
verb in the (a) sentences, and the non-Stative verb in the (b)
sentences.

(a) I am (called) Mary.   (b) S/he called me Mary.
Kofi has a car.   Kofi will get a car tomorrow.
I live in Accra.   I lived in Ho for two years.
She is pregnant.   She will become pregnant.
S/he is carrying a bag.   S/he carried the bag.

Lesson 26

INGRESSIVE FORMS OF THE VERB

Two prefixes, bɛ- and kɔ-, derived from the verbs 'ba' (come) and 'kɔ' (go) occur in some Tense/Aspect forms of the verb to indicate a movement towards or away from the speaker that occurs with the action indicated by the verb, as illustrated by the following sentences:

Kofi fa.	Kofi takes it.
Kofi bɛfa.	Kofi comes and takes it.
Kofi kɔfa.	Kofi goes and takes it.
Metɔnee.	I sold it.
Mebɛtɔnee.	I came and sold it.
Mekɔtɔnee.	I went and sold it.

These prefixes are said on low tone, and so it is possible to dinstinguish between the 'coming' Ingressive and the Simple Future forms of the verb. The Simple Future has a high tone prefix bɛ-.

ɔbɛ̀fá.	S/he comes and takes it.	ɔbɛ́fá.	S/he will take it.
ɔbɛ̀gyeʼ	S/he comes and receives it.	ɔbɛ́gyé.	S/he'll receive it.

The Stative, the Simple Future and the Immediate Future do not have Ingressive forms. The following are examples of Ingressive verbs in the different Tense/Aspect forms.

Habitual:	Mebɛtɔ wɔ ha.	I come and buy it here.
	Yɛkɔtɔ wɔ hɔ.	We go and buy it there.
	ɔnkɔtɔ wɔ hɔ.	S/he doesn't go and buy it there.
Progressive:	ɔrekɔtɔ.	S/he is going to buy it.
	ɔrebɛtɔ.	S/he is coming to buy it.
	ɔmmɛtɔ.	S/he's not coming to buy it.

(Note that the above Positive Progressive form of the 'coming' Ingressive is the same as the Immediate Future, but the Negative is different. The Negative Future is: ɔntɔ, S/he won't buy it.)

Past:	Yɛbɛhũĩ [yebehũĩ].	We came and saw it.
	ɔkɔhũĩ [okohũĩ].	S/he went and saw it.
	ɔankɔhũ [wankohũ].	S/he didn't go and see it.

Perfect:	Mabɛfa [mabɛfa].	I've come and taken it.
	Memmɛfae.	I haven't come and taken it.
	ɔakɔfa [wakɔfa].	S/he has gone and taken it.
Simple	Bɛpra ha.	Come and sweep here.
Imperative:	Kɔpra hɔ.	Go and sweep there.
	Nkɔpra hɔ.	Don't go and sweep there.
Optative	(ma) ɔmmɛbisa.	Let him come and ask.
Imperative:	(ma) ɔnkɔbisa.	Let him go and ask.
	(mma) ɔnnkɔbisa.	Don't let him go and ask.

(Note that the vowels of the prefixes for the verbs 'hû' and 'bisa' change as a result of vowel harmony.)

Consecutive:	(ɔbɛba) abɛfa akɔ.	S/he'll come and take it away (go).
	(ɔmma) mmɛfa nkɔ.	S/he won't come and take it away.
	(ɔbɛkɔ) akɔfa akɔ.	S/he'll go and take it away.
	(ɔnkɔ) nkɔfa nkɔ.	S/he won't go and take away.

EXERCISE

Give the 3rd person singular forms of the following verbs in both the
    a) coming-Ingressive
    b) going-Ingressive forms of the
Habitual, the Perfect and the Simple Imperative.

| da | sleep | hwɛ | look at |
| bu | break | gyina | stop / stand |

eg. fa: ɔkɔfa / ɔbɛfa.   S/he goes/comes and takes it.
        ɔakɔfa / ɔabɛfa.   S/he has gone/come and taken it.
        Kɔfa / bɛfa.   Go/come and take it.

Lesson 27

THE REDUPLICATED VERB

Reduplication is a type of compound-formation in which the whole or part of a stem is repeated. Reduplicated verbs often indicate repeated action, a plural subject or a plural object. Sometimes the reduplicated verbs have a slightly different shade of meaning from the original stem, as illustrated by the following examples.

kasa	to speak / talk	kasakasa	to keep speaking / to nag
bisa	to ask	bisebisa	to keep asking (also with plural subject / object)
tu	to dig up	tutu	to keep digging (also with plural object)
frɛ	to call	frɛfrɛ	to call (with plural object)
hwɛ	to look at	hwehwɛ	to look for / search
horo	to wash (clothes)	hohoro	to wash up
pa	to skim the surface	pepa	to wipe
da	to sleep	deda	to put (eg. a child) to sleep
di	to eat (with object)	didi	to eat (without object)

EXERCISE

Use the simple verb and its reduplicated form to make up sentences to illustrate the difference between them.

eg.	Kofi rekasa.	Kofi is speaking.
	Kofi rekasakasa.	Kofi is nagging /grumbling.
	Kɔfrɛ no.	Go and call him/her.
	Kɔfrɛfrɛ wɔn.	Go and call them.

Lesson 28

PHRASAL VERBS

The following are commonly used Phrasal Verbs made up of two verbs or a verb and a noun.

bɔ dam	be mad	gye di	believe (take eat)
bo nsã	to be drunk	kã kyerɛ	tell (say show)
di asɛm	to settle a case/judge	sɔ mu [som]	to hold
di agorɔ	to play	tena ase	to sit down
di atorɔ	to tell lies	to nnwom	to sing
di kan	to lead	tu mmirika	to run
di akyi(re)	to follow/be behind	tu kwan	to travel
di nkɔmɔ	to have a chat	tua ka	to pay
di kɔnkɔnsa	to tell lies/spread rumour	yɛ adeɛ	to do something
fa bra/brɛ	bring (take come)		admirable
fa kɔ	take away (take go)	yɛ dede	to make noise/
fa kyɛ	forgive (take give away)		be noisy

Where there are two verbs, these act as one verb in the Past positive forms of the verb. In the other forms of the verb, each verb inflects for the appropriate Tense / Aspect, as would normally happen in a serial verb construction.

ɔkã kyerɛɛ me.　S/he told me.　　Mekã kyerɛ no.　I tell him/her.
　(Past)　　　　　　　　　　　　(Hab)

ɔbɛkã akyerɛ me.　S/he'll tell me.　Makã akyerɛ no.　I've told him.
　(Fut)　　　　　　　　　　　　(Perf)

EXERCISE

Make up sentences of your own using any ten of the phrasal verbs in this lesson.

Lesson 29

NOUNS

SINGULAR AND PLURAL NOUNS

Twi nouns usually have a prefix, which may be a vowel e-, ɛ-, a-, o-, ɔ-, or the consonant m- or n- in the singular, and a-, m- or n- in the plural, plus an optional suffix -fo(ɔ) for nouns referring to humans. Some nouns also have a suffix -e, -ɛ, -o, or -ɔ as well.

efie	home	afie	homes
etuo	gun	atuo	guns
ɛdan	house / room	adan	houses / rooms
ɛboɔ	stone	aboɔ	stones
ɛba / ɔba	child	mma	children
ɔhene	chief	ahemfo	chiefs
ɔpanyin	elder	mpanyimfoɔ	elders
osikani	rich person	asikafoɔ	rich people
onipa	person / human being	nnipa	people
abofra	child / young person	mmofra	children
ataadeɛ	dress	ntaadeɛ	dresses
mpa	bed(s)		
nkateɛ	groundnuts		
nkrane	ants		
ntɛtea	(tiny) ants		
mfɔteɛ	termites		

Kinship nouns make their plurals by adding a suffix -nom.

nua	sibling	(a)nuanom
agya / papa	father	agyanom / papanom
ɛna / maame	mother	ɛnanom / maamenom
wɔfa	uncle	wɔfanom
nana	grandparent	nananom

EXERCISE

Make up plurals of
        a) kinship nouns
        b) non-kinship nouns of your choice,
qualifying them with any of the numbers from 2 to 15.

Lesson 30

NOUNS (cont'd)

Nominalization

The nominal prefixes e-, ɛ-, a-, o-, ɔ-, m-, n-, the nominal suffixes -e, -ɛ, -o, -ɔ, and the agentive suffix -ni / -foɔ are used to make nouns from verbs and adjectives.

hĩã	to be in need	ohĩã	poverty
		ohĩãni	a poor person
		ahĩãfoɔ	poor people
kyea	to greet	nkyea	greeting
didi	to eat	adidie	eating
brɛ	to be tired	ɔbrɛ	tiredness
dware	to have a bath	adwareɛ	bathing
wo	to give birth	awoɔ	childbearing
fe	to throw up	ɛfeɛ	vomit
wu	to die	owuo	death
bu	to respect	obuo	respect
da	to sleep	nna	sleep
dɔ	to love	ɔdɔ	love
dɔ	to weed / farm	adɔ	weeding / farming
tan	to hate	ɔtan	hatred
kɛse	big	ɔkɛseɛ	a big person
		akɛsefoɔ	big people
tuntum	black	atuntum	the black ones

Phrasal verbs made up of verb and noun are often nominalized by compound formation in which the verb and noun are reversed.

da ase	to thank	aseda	thanks
di nkɔmɔ	to converse	nkɔmɔdie	conversation
di asɛm	to judge	asenni	judging
di agorɔ	to play	agodie	playing/playfulness
to nnwom	to sing	nnwomtoɔ	singing
tena ase	to sit / settle down	asetena	living condition
tu kwan	to travel	akwantuo	travelling
tu mmirika	to run	mmirikatuo	running / race
tua ka	to pay	akatua	salary / reward / punishment

eg. Yɛnni aseda.　　　　"We don't owe each other thanks.

ɔpɛ agodie dodo.　　　　S/he is too playful / likes playing too much.

Ne nnwomtoɔ yɛ me dɛ.　I like (enjoy) her singing.

Asetena mu ayɛ den.　　Life (living condition) has become difficult.

EXERCISE

a) Learn the new nouns in this lesson.
b) Make up sentences with any ten of them.

The Dimunitive / Feminine suffix

There's a suffix pronounced variously as ba / wa / ma / a which occurs with various nouns to indicate a smaller or a feminine version, as in the examples below.

kuro	town	akuraa	village
dadeɛ	iron / metal	dadewa /dadowa	nail(s)
ɔbaa	woman / female	abaawa	maidservant
		ababaawa	young woman
		abaayewa	young girl
ɔbarima	man / male	abarimawa	boy
[ɔbɛɛma]		[abɛɛmowa]	
owura	sir	awuraa	lady
Ata	male twin	Ataa	female twin
ɛseɛ	father	sewaa	aunt (father's sister)
ɔsɛɛ	a man's name	Sɛɛwaa	a woman's name
Frempɔn	a man's name	Frempɔmaa	a woman's name

106

Lesson 31

ADJECTIVES AND ADVERBS

Adjectives

Adjectives follow the nouns they qualify, as in the following examples:

onipa pa	a good person	ataadeɛ fɛɛfɛ bi	a beautiful dress
ɔbaa tietia	a short woman	ɔkraman ketewa	a small dog

A large number of adjectives in English are rendered by verbs in Twi.

eg. biri	to be black	ɔbiri [obiri].	S/he is black.
fɛre	to be shy	Kofi fɛre adeɛ.	Kofi is shy.
sua	to be small	Amma sua dodo.	Amma is too small.

Some adjectives may be doubled (reduplicated) for intensity.

eg. papa	good	papapapa/papaapa	very good
fɛ	beautiful	fɛfɛɛfɛ	very beautiful
tia	short	tietia	very short
tenten	long/tall	tenteenten	very long/tall
ketewa	small	ketekete	very small
		keteketekete	very, very tiny
hye	hot	hyehyeehye	very hot

Adverbs

Adverbs modify the verbs they follow. In the examples below, the adverbs are italicised.

ɔbaa *ntɛm*.	S/he came quickly / early.
Papa yi kasa *dodo*.	This man talks too much.
ɔnante *brɛoo*.	S/he walks slowly.
ɛnyɛ fɛ *koraa*.	It is not nice at all.
Nom no *nkakrankakra*.	Drink it a little at a time (little by little).
Mɛyɛ no *fɛfɛɛfɛ*.	I will do it nicely.
ɔkura mu *denneenen*.	S/he is holding it firmly.

107

As can be seen from the last two sentences, the 'tripled' form of the adjective may also function as an adverb.

Like adjectives, adverbs may also be reduplicated for intensity.

pɛ	exactly	pɛpɛɛpɛ	with precision	
ntɛm	quickly	ntɛntɛm	very quickly	ntɛntɛɛntɛm
				very very quickly

EXERCISE

1. Make up ten sentences, five with the simple adjective, and five with the reduplicated adjective.
2. Make up five sentences using any five of the adverbs in the sentences above.

Lesson 32

PRONOUNS

Pronouns

	Singular		Plural	
1st pers.	me	I	yɛn	we
2nd pers.	wo	you	mo	you
3rd pers.	ɔno	he/she/it (animate)	wɔɔnom/	they
	ɛno	it (non-animate)	ɔɔmo/wɔn/	
			yɛn	(many Asante speakers use 'yɛn' for both 'we' and 'they')

As has already been illustrated, Subject, Object and Possessive Pronouns are derived from these pronouns. It may be noted here, however, that the above 3rd person singular pronoun forms are used in emphatic sentences, as in the following examples.

| ɔno kɔ hɔ. | S/he (emphatic) goes there. |
| ɛno kɔ hɔ. | That particular one (eg. a bus) goes there. |

| Kofi de maa ɔno. | Kofi gave it to him/her in particular. |
| Kofi faa ɛno. | Kofi took that particular one. |

Subject pronouns

Non-emphatic subject pronouns are often not the full form of the pronouns listed above. They are usually prefixed to the verb, and, apart from 'wɔɔnom', they agree with the vowel of the verb in vowel harmony.

me-kɔ	I go	yɛ-di [yedi]	we eat it
wo-kɔ	you go	mo-di [mudi]	you eat it
ɔ-kɔ	s/he it (eg. a dog) goes	wɔɔnom di/	they eat it
ɛ-kɔ	it (eg. a car) goes	wɔ-di [wodi]	they eat it
		yɛ-di [yedi]	they eat it

Object pronouns

| ɔhwɛ me. | S/he looks at me. | ɔhwɛ yɛn. | S/he looks at us. |
| ɔfrɛ wo. | S/he calls you (sg.). | ɔfrɛ mo. | S/he calls you (plu). |

109

ɔhwɛ nʊ. S/he looks at him/her. ɔhwɛ wɔn/ S/he looks at them.

ɔhwɛ.   S/he looks at it.   wɔɔnom.

    (eg. a house)

Note that there is no overt object pronoun for non-animate objects.

EXERCISE

Express the following in Twi. Here are two examples:

    (I) thank you (sing./ plu.)   Meda wo / mo ase.
    Please (I beg you)   Mepa wo / mo kyɛw.

    They thank you (sing./ plu.).
    We thank him / them.
    Ask them / us / him.
    He's calling you / me / us.
    He sees you / me / them / it.
    They beg him.
    We beg you (sing. / plu.).
    He begs them.

Lesson 33

PRONOUNS (cont'd)

Possessive pronouns

me dan	my room / house	yɛn hene	our chief
wo twenee	your drum	mo nsã	your drink
ne ti	his/her/its head	wɔɔnom dan	their room

Changes occur in the tone of the possessive pronouns and also in the nouns they occur with :

		mè ǹsá	my hand
		mé dán	my house
àdàmfò	friend	màdámfò	my friend

The best way to learn the tone patterns of the possessive and other Twi expressions is to listen carefully to the tape that comes with this course book. Those with a background in Linguistics may refer to Chapter 3 of *The Akan Language: Its Sound Systems and Tonal Structure* (Dolphyne 1988, Ghana Universities Press, Accra).

Singular possessive pronouns and the first person plural possessive pronoun use a contracted form when followed by a noun beginning with a vowel:

m'adamfo	my friend	BUT	mo adamfo	your friend
w'ani	your eyes		mo ani	your eyes
n'adwuma	his/her work		wɔɔnom /	their work
n'ani	its eyes		yɛn adwuma	
y'adamfo	our friend			

EXERCISE

Use the possessive pronouns with the following nouns:

(ɛ)sě	teeth	asõ	ear(s)
(e)kuro	town	(ɛ)nan	leg
akuraa	village (small town)	(e)fie	home
(ɛ)dan	house / room	(ɔ)hene	chief

Note that apart from the prefix a-, noun prefixes are deleted in possessive constructions. This is why they are

111

enclosed in brackets in the examples above.

Where the possessor noun is expressed, it comes first in the noun phrase, just like the possessive pronoun.

Kofi ti	Kofi's head	Abena tikya	Abena's teacher
papa bi dan	a certain man's house	Yaw sika	Yaw's money
maame no ba	the woman's child	Amma ataadeɛ	Amma's dress

Lesson 34

OTHER GRAMMATICAL ITEMS

Articles

no	the	eg.	ɔkraman no	the dog
			papa no	the man
			atadeɛ no	the dress
			kaa no	the car
bi	a / an /		ɔkraman bi	a (certain) dog
	a certain		papa bi	a (certain) man
			atadeɛ bi	a dress
			kaa bi	a (certain) car
			da bi	one day

'Prepositions'

The equivalent of English prepositions are nouns which occur *after* other nouns, and therefore sometimes called 'postpositions'.

aseɛ	the under part	eg.	ɛpono no ase	under the table
			dua no ase	under the tree
			paati no ase	at the party
ɛso	the top		ɛpono no so	on (top of) the table
			dua no so	on top of the tree
			mpa no so	on the bed
anim	front (face)		ɛdan no anim	in front of the house
			adaka no anim	in front of the box
			ɛpono no anim	in front of the table
akyi(re)	back		ɛdan no akyi	behind the house/ building
			ɛpono no akyi	behind the table
			mpa no akyi	behind the bed
ɛhɔ̃	outside (body)		ɛdan no hɔ̃	outside / around the house
			mpa no hɔ̃	around / near the bed
emu	inside (often pronounced 'm')		ɛdan no mu [ɛdan num]	inside the house/building
			adaka no mu	inside the box
			edwa no mu	inside the market
ɛnkyɛn	side		ɛpono no nkyɛn	beside the table
			mpa no nkyɛn	by the bed

113

Dialogue 30

Kofi:	Amma ɛte sɛn?	Amma how is it?
Amma:	ɛyɛ. Na wo nso ɛ?	Fine. And you?
Kofi:	Oh, ɛyɛ ara.	Oh, it is a bit fine.
Amma:	Adɛn?	Why / What is it?
Kofi:	Amma m'ani abere.	Amma, I'm hot.
	Menhũ me buuku, nso	I can't find my book, yet
	ɔkyena mewɔ nsɔhwɛ.	I have an examination tomorrow
Amma:	Woahwehwɛ [wahwehwɛ] wo dan mu yiye?	Have you searched your (inside your) room thoroughly?
Kofi:	Aane. Mahwehwɛ me pono no so,	I've searched (for it) on my table
	mahwehwɛ m'adaka mu ɛne	I've looked inside my box and
	me mpa ase, nso ɛnni hɔ.	under my bed, but it is not there.
Amma:	Woahwehwɛ wo pono no akyi?	Have you looked behind your table?
	Ebia afiri atɔ akyire.	Perhaps it has fallen at the back.
Kofi:	Menhwɛɛ hɔ.	I haven't looked (for it) there.
	Seesei deɛ merekɔ (meekɔ) laibri	Right now I'm going to the library.
	mesan ba me dan mu a mɛhwɛ hɔ.	When I return to my room, I'll look (for it) there.
Amma:	ɛnneɛ akyire yi yɛbɛhyia.	See you later.
Kofi:	Yoo.	All right.

EXERCISE

List the prepositional phrases in the dialogue, and use them in sentences of your own.

Lesson 35

OTHER GRAMMATICAL ITEMS (cont'd)

Conjunctions

ne (for individual items)	and	eg. Kofi ne Amma ɔne me kɔe.	Kofi and Amma S/he and I went.
na (for clauses)	and	ɔbaa ha na ɔbɛfaeɛ.	S/he came here and took it.
		Mɛkɔ na masan aba ɔkyena.	I'll go and I'll (turn) come back tomorrow.
sɛ	that	ɔkãã sɛ ɔbɛba.	S/he said that s/he will come.
		Ka kyerɛ no sɛ mahũ.	Tell him/her that I've found it.
efisɛ	because	ɔkɔhũũ [okohũũ] dɔkta efisɛ ɔyare.	S/he went and saw a doctor because s/he was ill.
		Mayɛ komm efisɛ m'ani kom.	I'm quiet because I'm sleepy.
enti	because of/ therefore	Kofi nti na mebaeɛ.	It is because of Kofi that I came.
		Mahũ pɛn enti mensuro [minsuro].	I've seen it before therefore I'm not afraid.
		ɔyare nti na ɔayɛ dinn.	S/he is ill, that is why s/he is quiet
(na)nso	but	Mepɛ, nanso menni sika.	I like it but I don't have money.
		ɔyare nso ɔbɛba.	S/he is ill, but s/he'll come.
ebia	maybe	Bisa no ebia ɔwɔ bi.	Ask him/her, maybe s/he has some.
		Mɛtwɛn no, ebia ɔbɛba.	I'll wait for him/her, maybe s/he'll come.
a	clause marker for relative and other subordinate clauses	Papa no a ɔbaeɛ no... Nhoma a wotɔeɛ no...	The man who came... The book that you bought...
		Mekɔ me dan mu a mɛhwehwɛ.	When I go to my room, I'll look for it.

115

		(Sɛ) ɔba a mɛbisa no.	(If)/when s/he comes, I'll ask him/her.
sɛ...a	if	Sɛ mehũ a mede bɛba.	If I find it, I'll bring it.
		Sɛ Kofi ba a mɛka akyerɛ no.	If Kofi comes, I'll tell him.
sɛ...o	whether ..or not	Sɛ ɔba o sɛ ɔamma o ɛnyɛ m'asɛm.	Whether s/he comes or does not come, it is none of my business.
kyɛn/ sen	than	Kofi sõ kyɛn/sen Amma.	Kofi is bigger than Amma.
		Kofi nsõ nkyɛn/ nsen Amma.	Kofi isn't bigger than Amma.
		Amma yɛ tenten kyɛn/sen me.	Amma is taller than me.
		Amma nyɛ tenten nkyɛn/nsen me.	Amma is not taller than me.
		Amma kyɛn me tenten.	Amma is taller than me.
		Amma nkyɛn me tenten.	Amma is not taller than me.
		Ataadeɛ no sua kyɛn/sen wei.	That dress is smaller than this one
		Ataadeɛ no nsua nkyɛn/nsen wei.	That dress is not smaller than this one.

Notes on kyɛn/sen

1. 'kyɛn' is used on its own as a verb to mean 'to surpass', 'to be greater than', as in the sentence
   Amma kyɛn me tenten. : Amma is taller than me.
   'sen' can also be used in the same context, but 'kyɛn' is the word that is usually preferred.
2. Both 'kyɛn' and 'sen' on their own imply a greater or better quality. It is therefore not possible to use either 'kyɛn' or 'sen' its own in the sentence
   Ataadeɛ no sua kyɛn/sen wei. : That dress is smaller than this one.
   where the item compared is considered 'inferior'.
3. In the negative sentences, 'kyɛn' and 'sen' behave like verbs in taking the negative prefix n-.

EXERCISE

Make up two sentences with each of the conjunctions.

Dialogue 31

Amma: Kofi ɛte sɛn?	Kofi how are you?
Kofi: Ɛyɛ. Na wo nso ɛ?	Fine, and you?
Amma: Ɛyɛ. Na kaa yi ɛ?	Fine. And how about this car?
Kofi: Kaa wei, ɛyɛ me wɔfa kaa.	This car? It is my uncle's car.
Amma: Wo wɔfa a ɔkɔ America no?	Your uncle who has gone to America?.
Kofi: Aane, ɔrekɔ [ɔɔkɔ] na ɔde gyaa me maame.	Yes. It was when he was going that he left it with my mother.
Amma: Wonim [wunim] kaa kã?	Do you know how to drive?
Kofi: Aane, mewɔ laesens dadaada.	Yes, I've had a license a long time ago.
Sɛ menni [minni] bi a ankã me maame mfa kaa yi safoa mma me.	If I didn't have one, my mother won't give me the key to this car.
Amma: Ɛsɛ sɛ mebisa [mibisa] efisɛ ebinom kã kaa a wɔnni [wonni] laesens.	It is proper that I ask, because some people drive when they don't have a license.
Kofi: Me ne Yaw gyee laesens da ko(ro).	I and Yaw got our license the same (on one) day.
Amma: Saa? Nso menhũũ [minhũũ] sɛ worekã [wookã] kaa da.	Is that so? But I haven't seen you drive before (ever).
Kofi: Ɛnneɛ tena ase na memfa wo nkɔ fie.	Then sit down and let me take you home.

Vocabulary

gya	to leave/hand over responsibility to
kã kaa	to drive
safoa	key
ɛsɛ	it is proper / necessary
ɛsɛ sɛ woba	you have to come (it is essential that you come)
ebinom	some people (plural of 'obi': somebody)
da	ever / before
makɔ hɔ da	I've gone there before

EXERCISE

List the conjunctions in the dialogue, and use them in sentences of your own.

117

Lesson 36

OTHER GRAMMATICAL ITEMS (cont'd)

Emphatic particles

Note: The subject pronoun is repeated after the particle.

deɛ	in particular	eg.	Me deɛ menkɔ.	I in particular won't go.
			Kofi deɛ ɔpɛ fufuo.	As for Kofi he likes fufu.
			Ataadeɛ yi deɛ ɛnyɛ fɛ.	This dress in particular is not nice.
na			Me na mebaeɛ.	It is I who came.
			Kofi na ɔbɛyɛ.	It is Kofi who will do it.
nkőăǎ	only		ɔno nkőăǎ na ɔbaeɛ.	It is only s/he who came.
			Kofi nkőăǎ na ɔbɛyɛ.	It is Kofi alone who will do it.
			Amma nkőăǎ na ɔkɔ hɔ.	It is only Amma who goes there.
pɛ	only (normally used with numbers)		Nnipa du pɛ na ɛbaeɛ.	Only ten people came.
			Baakő pɛ na ɛwɔ ha.	It is only one that is here.
mpo/ koraa	even		Amma mpo/koraa bɛtumi ayɛ.	Even Amma can do it.
			Kaa no mpo/koraa asɛe.	The car is even spoilt.
ankasa (emphasising identity)			Kofi ankasa kɔɔ hɔ.	Kofi himself went there.

Demonstrative pronouns

					Plural
yei / wei	this	eg.	adeɛ wei	this thing	nneɛma wei
			ɔbaa wei	this woman	mmaa weinom
yi	this		adeɛ yi	this thing	nneɛma yi
			abofra yi	this child	mmofra yi
no	that		adeɛ no	the/that thing	nneɛma no
			ɔhene no	that chief	ahemfo no

EXERCISE

Make up two sentences with each of the emphatic particles and the demonstrative pronouns.

Some common idiomatic expressions with body part words

1. Eyes : ani
    a) ani abere : eyes are red
    i.e. one is in difficulty; under pressure to do something; has lost something valuable, etc.
    eg. M'ani abere. : I'm in distress; under stress and don't have time for anything else.
    Kofi ani abere. : Kofi is under stress.

    b) ani bere adeɛ : eyes are red for something
    i.e. to be envious
    eg. Kofi ani bere adeɛ. : Kofi is envious of what others have.
    Noun : aniberee

    c) ani asɔ : eyes have accepted
    i.e. to be appreciative eg. of a present; a kind deed.
    eg. M'ani asɔ : I am happy about it; I appreciate what has been done.
    eg. N'ani nsɔ adeɛ. : S/he is disrespectful.
    (note negative prefix in nsɔ)

    d) ani agye : eyes have received
    i.e. to be happy
    eg. m'ani agye : I am happy.
    Kofi ani agye paa : Kofi is very happy.
    Yɛgyee Kofi ani : We made Kofi happy / We entertained him.
    Noun : anigyee

    e) ani atra ntɔn : eyes have jumped over eyebrow
    i.e. to be disrespectful, rude or saucy.
    eg. N'ani atra ne ntɔn : S/he is rude / cheeky.

    f) ani yɛ den : eyes are hard
    i.e. to be tough; persistent
    eg. Kofi ani yɛ den/ : Kofi is tough / a hard nut to crack.
    Kofi ani ɛ den.
    Noun : aniɛden

Note how the verb yε can be reduced to a vowel in this and similar expressions when it occurs with an adjective.

g) anim agu ase : the face has fallen down
   i.e. to have disgraced one's self; no longer worthy of respect.
   eg. W'anim agu ase. : You have disgraced yourself / lost all respect.
       Yεagu n'anim ase.: They have disgraced him/her / s/he has been disgraced.
   Noun : animguaseε

h) ani awu : eyes are dead
   i.e. to be ashamed because of bad behaviour/speech, etc.
   eg. Amma ani awu enti ɔremma ha bio. : Amma is ashamed (of what she did) so she won't come here again.
   Noun : aniwuo

i) ani da so : eyes are set (lay) on (it)
   i.e. to hope / expect
   eg. M'ani da so sε ɔbεba.: I expect (have hopes) that s/he will come.
   Noun : anidasoɔ

j) ani so yε hye : the surface of the eyes are hot
   i.e. to be headstrong
   eg. Amma ani so yε hye dodo./ : Amma is too headstrong.
       Amma ani so ɔ hye dodo.
   Noun : anisoɔhyeε

2. Head : eti(re)
   a) ti awu : head is dead
      i.e. to be unintelligent
      eg. Ne ti awu. : S/he is not clever.
      Noun : tiwuiε

   b) ti bɔne : bad head
      i.e. ill luck
      eg. Wo yε ti bɔne. : You are an 'ill luck' person.
   c) ti(ri) yε : head is good
      i.e. to be lucky
      ti(ri) nyε : head is not good
      i.e. to be unlucky

120

eg. Wo ti(ri) yɛ. : You are lucky.
    Ne ti(ri) nyɛ. : S/he is unlucky.

d) tiri mu yɛ den : inside the head is hard
   i.e. to be wicked; unfeeling
   eg. Kofi tiri mu yɛ den / : Kofi is wicked.
       Kofi tiri mu ɔ den.
   Noun : atirimuɔden

e) tiri mu yɛ sum : inside the head is dark
   i.e. to be wicked in a criminal sense
   eg. Ne tiri mu yɛ sum / : S/he is wicked / scheming.
       Ne tiri mu o sum.

f) tiri mu yɛ : inside the head is good
   i.e. to be considerate, thoughtful of others
   eg. Amma tiri mu yɛ paa. : Amma is very caring.

g) tiri nkwa : life to your head
   i.e. congratulations
   eg. Amma, wo tiri nkwa. : Congratulations, Amma!
   response : Me tiri da ase. : My head thanks you / thank you.

3. Brain / mind : adwene
   a) sɛe adwene : to spoil the mind
      i.e. to poison one's mind
      eg. N'adwene asɛe wɔ me ho.: His mind is spoilt about
                                    me / he thinks ill of me.
          ɔasɛe Amma adwene. :   S/he has poisoned Amma's
                                    mind.

   b) adwene sua : to have a small brain
      i.e. not mature
      eg. Woadwene sua. : You are not mature / you think like a
                          child.

   c) ha adwene : to disturb the mind
      i.e. to be troublesome
      eg. Abofra yi ha adwene. : This child is troublesome.
          Wo ha adwene dodo. : You are too troublesome.

4. Ear : asŏ
   a) asŏ yɛ den : the ear is hard
      i.e. to be stubborn
      eg. Kofi asŏ yɛ den./ : Kofi is stubborn.

121

Kofi asõ ɔ den.
Amma asõ nyɛ den.: Amma is not stubborn.
Noun : asõɔden

b) asõ yɛ mmerɛ : the ear is soft
i.e. to be obedient (not as commonly used as asõɔden)
eg. N'asõ yɛ mmerɛ./ : S/he is obedient.
N'asõ ɔ mmerɛ.

5. Nose : hwene
hwene mu bɔn : inside the nose smells
i.e. to be snobbish
eg. Nɛ hwene mu bɔn no. : S/he is snobbish.

6. Mouth : ano
a) ano mu yɛ dɛ : inside the mouth is sweet
i.e. to have a sweet tooth
eg. Amma ano mu yɛ no dɛ. : Amma is sweet-toothed.
Noun : anomuɔdɛ

b) ano yɛ den : the mouth is hard
i.e. to be tough and loud-spoken, and always have the
last say
eg. Amma ano yɛ den/ : Amma is 'loud'.
Amma ano ɔ den.
Noun : anoɔden

c) ano yɛ mmerɛ : the mouth is soft
i.e. to be polite and soft-spoken
eg. Ma w'ano nyɛ mmerɛ. : Be soft spoken and don't insist
on your point of view.
(Note : ma ....(ɛ)nyɛ is the Optative Imperative form.)

d) ano yɛ toro : the mouth is slippery
i.e. unable to keep a secret
(hence Ghanaian slang : 'okro mouth')
eg. Kofi ano yɛ toro / : Kofi cannot keep a secret.
Kofi ano ɔ toro.

7. Teeth : ɛsě
ɛsě afem : teeth are set on edge
i.e. to be embarrassed or rendered speechless because
of an awkward situation created by another person.

eg. Woama me sɛ̃ afem. : <small>You have embarrassed me / made me speechless.</small>

8. Tongue : tɛkrɛma / kɛtrɛma
       tɛkrɛma yɛ dɛ : to have a sweet tongue
       i.e. to be good at flattery / to be persuasive
       eg. Wo tɛkrɛma yɛ dɛ. / : <small>You know how to flatter /</small>
           Wo tɛkrɛma ɛ dɛ.   <small>persuade. (i.e. I know you're saying all this to please me)</small>

9. Chest : koko
       koko yɛ duru : the chest is heavy
       i.e. to be brave
       eg. Kofi koko yɛ du(ru)./ : <small>Kofi is brave.</small>
           Kofi koko o du(ru).
           Amma koko nyɛ duru. : <small>Amma is not brave.</small>
       Noun : akokuoduro

10. Stomach : yafunu / yam(u)
       a) yamu yɛ : inside the stomach is good
          i.e. to be kind
          eg. Amma yamu yɛ. : <small>Amma is kind / generous.</small>
          Noun : ayam(u)ye

       b) yamu yɛ nwono : inside the stomach is sour / bitter
          i.e. not generous / miserly
          eg. Amma yamu yɛ nwono / : <small>Amma is not generous.</small>
             Amma yamu ɔ nwono.
          Noun : ayamuɔnwono

11. Hand : nsa
       a) nsa yɛ den : the hand (palm) is hard
          i.e. to be stingy / not generous with money
          eg. Kofi nsa yɛ den / : <small>Kofi is stingy.</small>
             Kofi nsa ɛ den.

       b) nsa go : the hand (palm) is soft
          i.e. to be generous with money
          eg. Kofi nsa go. / : <small>Kofi is generous with money.</small>

Some common Akan names and their meanings

Not all Akan names have clearly defined meanings. However, apart from the names relating to the day on which one is born, there are also names that relate to the circumstances of one's birth. These have meaning. The following are some of them.

Piesie   first born child (one who sprouts 'pie' out of the anthill 'sie', like a mushroom; i.e. the one who opens the womb)

Manu (M) Maanu (F)	second born child	eg. Kofi Manu Afia Maanu
Mensa (M) Mansa (F)	third born child	eg. Kwadwo Mensa Adwoa Mansa
Anane	fourth born child	eg. Kwabena Anane Abena Anane
Num	fifth born child	(not in common use)
Nsĩa	sixth born child	eg. Kwaku Nsĩa Akua Nsĩa
Nsonwaa	seventh born child	eg. Kwadwo Nsonwaa Adwoa Nsonwaa

(eighth born child - not in use)

Nkroma	ninth born child	eg. Kwame Nkroma Ama Nkroma
Badu	tenth born child	eg. Yaw Badu Yaa Badu
Dukɔ	eleventh born child	eg. Kwaku Dukɔ Akua Dukɔ
Dunu	twelfth born child	eg. Kwabena Dunu Abena Dunu

Ata (M)	twin	eg.	Kwasi Ata/
Ataa (F)			Ata Kwasi
			Akosua Ataa/
			Ataa Akosua

Ata / Ataa Panyin   elder twin
Atakuma/ Ataa Kumaa   younger twin
Obiwom   younger twin
(obi: somebody; wɔ: is; mu: inside)

| Tawia | child born after twins | eg. | Kwame Tawia |
| | | | Amma Tawia |

Nyankomago	child born after Tawia	eg.	Kwaku
			Nyankomago
Adae	child born on Adae	eg.	Akosua Adae
	festival day		

Fɔdwoɔ (Monday)   names for children born on
Fookuo (Wednesday)   other festive days in the
Fofie (Friday)   40-day cycle for reckoning the
Dapaa (Tuesday/Saturday)   Adae festival.

Nyamekyɛ   a gift from God; usually given to a first child, especially if the mother had almost given up hopes of having a child.

Nyameama   what God has given (...no man can take away); usually given to a child who was premature or who was very sickly as a baby.

Obimpɛ   somebody doesn't want you; usually given to a child whose father refuses reponsibility for the pregnancy, and therefore has no father.

Yɛmpɛw   we don't want you. (same circumstances as for Obimpɛ)

Adiyea   you've suffered grief; a child who loses a parent during infancy.

The following names are given to a child who survives after its mother had lost two or three babies. It is believed that if the child is given a horrible name, it will be rejected by its mother in the ancestral world, and will therefore remain in this world and not die.

Dɔnkɔ	slave
Asaseasã	there's no ground left (...to bury you)
Sumina	rubbish heap
Yɛmpɛw	we don't want you

Note

All the above names are not considered 'real' or 'proper' names. Every Akan child is given a 'real' name on the eighth day of its birth or soon after that day. The name given will be the name of a respected relation (dead or alive) usually from the father's family. Many of such names have male and female versions, and they normally have no meaning.

Male / Female

Opoku / Pokuaa

ɔsɛe / Sɛɛwaa

Asante / Asantewaa

Agyei / Agyeewaa

Dɛe / Dɛɛwaa

Safo / Safoaa

Adutwum / Adutwûwaa

Werɛkõ / Werɛkõãã

ɔpɔn / Pɔmaa

Oduro / Durowaa

Kwaaten / Kwaatemaa

Ofosu / Fosuaa

APPENDIX III

Proverbs

The use of appropriate or relevant proverbs in one's speech is considered a mark of eloquence. A few common proverbs are given below. The first eight are also used as names for certain wax prints. Usually, though not always, the main noun in the proverb refers to the motif in the wax print.

1. Woafa me nwa.
   You have caught me like you would catch a snail, without effort.
   i.e. I have become an easy prey for you / you have taken advantage of me.

2. Dua baakɔ gye mframa a ɛbu.
   If one tree alone stands in the path of the wind, it falls.
   i.e. One person should not take on everybody's responsibilities, especially in the extended family.

3. Anoma antu a ɔbua da.
   If a bird does not fly, it starves.
   i.e. Nothing ventured, nothing gained.

4. Ahwene pa nkasa.
   Precious beads do not rattle (make no noise).
   i.e. Empty barrels make the most noise.

5. Borɔferɛ a ɛyɛ dɛ na abaa da aseɛ.
   It is the pawpaw/papaya tree that bears sweet fruit which has a stick under it.
   i.e. You can tell a person's position / character by his/her appearance.

6. Kɔnkɔnsani bɛbrɛ.
   The gossip/one who tells stories about others, will suffer in life.

7. Owuo atwereɛ, baako mforo.
   Death's ladder is not just for one person to climb.
   i.e. We will all die (so do not behave as if you are immortal).

127

8. Ohuruɛ si akyekyereɛ akyi a, ɔsi hɔ kwa.
   If the tsetse fly is standing on the back of the tortoise (in the hope of sucking its blood) it is wasting its time.
   i.e. You can't touch or hurt me.

9. Akokɔba a ɔbɛn oni na ɔdi abɛbɛ srɛ.
   The chick which is always near its mother gets the thigh (the best part) of the grasshopper.
   i.e. Out of sight, out of mind.

10. Aboa bi bɛka wo a na ɔfiri wo ntoma mu.
    An insect that bites you will surely be hiding inside your cloth.
    i.e. The person closest to you is the one who can hurt you most.

11. Kwaterekwa se ɔbɛma wo ntoma a tie ne din.
    If a naked man says he will give you cloth to wear don't believe him.
    (Kwaterekwa : stark naked)

12. Aboa a ɔnni dua, Onyame na ɔpra ne hɔ.
    It is God who drives away flies from the back of the animal that has no tail.
    i.e. God takes care of the destitute.

13. Sɛnea w'awofo ahwɛ wo ama wo sɛ afifiri no, ɛsɛ sɛ wohwɛ wɔn ma wɔɔnom deɛ tutu.
    Just as your parents have looked after you for your teeth to grow, you must look after them for theirs to fall out.
    i.e. Children have an obligation to take care of their old parents.

14. Obi nkyerɛ abofra Nyame.
    Nobody teaches a child about God.
    i.e. There are certain facts of life or certain situations that are very obvious.

15. Nsa kɔ na nsa aba.
    Hand go, hand come.
    i.e. There is (or should be) reciprocity in every relationship.

16. Benkum dware nifa, na nifa adware benkum.
    The left hand bathes the right, the right hand bathes the left.
    Same as (15): You scratch my back, I scratch yours.

APPENDIX IV

A limited English-Twi vocabulary

Numbers

1	baakõ	44	aduanan nan
2	mmienu	45	aduanan num
3	mmeɛnsã	47	aduanan nson
4	(ɛ)nan	48	aduanan nwɔtwe
5	(e)num	50	aduonum
6	(e)nsĩã	51	aduonum baakõ
7	(ɛ)nson	52	aduonum mmienu
8	nwɔtwe	53	aduonum mmeɛnsã
9	(ɛ)nkron	56	aduonum nsĩã
10	(e)du	59	aduonum nkron
11	du baakõ	60	aduosĩã
12	du mmienu	64	aduosĩã nan
13	du mmeɛnsã	70	aduɔson
14	du nan	72	aduɔson mmienu
15	du num	78	aduɔson nwɔtwe
16	du nsĩã	80	aduɔwɔtwe
17	du nson	81	aduɔwɔtwe baakõ
18	du nwɔtwe	90	aduɔkron
19	du nkron	95	aduɔkron num
20	aduonu	101	ɔha ne baakõ
21	aduonu baakõ	109	ɔha ne nkron
22	aduonu mmienu	110	ɔha ne du
23	aduonu mmeɛnsã	111	ɔha ne du baakõ
24	aduonu nan	115	ɔha ne du num
25	aduonu num	120	ɔha ne aduonu
26	aduonu nsĩã	124	ɔha ne aduonu nan
27	aduonu nson	128	ɔha ne aduonu nwɔtwe
28	aduonu nwɔtwe	130	ɔha ne aduasã
29	aduonu nkron	132	ɔha ne aduasã mmienu
30	aduasã	140	ɔha ne aduanan
31	aduasã baakõ	143	ɔha ne aduanan mmeɛnsã
34	aduasã nan	150	ɔha ne aduonum
37	aduasã nson	154	ɔha ne aduonum nan
39	aduasã nkron	160	ɔha ne aduosĩã
40	aduanan	170	ɔha ne aduɔson
41	aduanan baakõ	180	ɔha ne aduɔwɔtwe

190	ɔha ne aduɔkron	600	ahansĩã
192	ɔha ne aduɔkron mmienu	700	ahanson
200	ahaanu	800	ahanwɔtwe
201	ahaanu ne baakɔ	900	ahankron
250	ahaanu aduonum	1000	apem
254	ahaanu aduonum naᴿ	1004	apem ne nan
300	ahaasã	1215	apem ahaanu du num
321	ahaasã aduonu baakɔ	1995	apem ahankron aduɔkron nu
400	ahanan	2010	mpem mmienu ne du
500	ahanum		

once	prɛkõ
twice	mprenu
three times	mprɛnsã
four times	mprɛnan
five times	mprenum
seven times	mprɛnson
ten times	mpredu
twenty times	mprɛ aduonu
forty times	mprɛ aduanan
a hundred times	mprɛ ɔha

first	(nea) edi kan
second	(nea) ɛtɔ so mmienu
third	(nea) ɛtɔ so mmeɛnsã
fourth	(nea) ɛtɔ so nan
fiftieth	(nea) ɛtɔ so aduonum
hundredth	(nea) ɛtɔ so ɔha

Words

A

able	tumi	annoy	hyɛ abufuo
abound/		answer (v)	bua
be plentiful	dɔɔsõ	answer (n)	mmuaeɛ
absent, be	ni hɔ	ant	tɛtea/nkrane
abuse/insult	yɛ	anthill	esie
accept	gye	any	biara/biaa
achieve	yɛ adeɛ	anybody	obiara/obiaa
acquire/obtain	nya	anyone	obiara
add	(de / fa) kã hõ	anything	biri-biara
address	kasa kyerɛ	any time	bere biara
adjudicate	di asɛm	anywhere	baa-biara
admit	gye to mu	apologise	pa kyɛw
advise	tu fo	apology	kyɛwpa
afford/	tumi tɔ	appeal/beg	srɛ
(able to buy)		appear/	pue
afraid, be	suro	come out	
again	(e)bio	appreciate	ani gye hõ
agree	pene		(be happy about)
agriculture	kua / kuayɛ	approach/see	hũ
aid/help	boa	get close	pini / twi bɛn
air	mframa	approve	pene
alcohol	nsã	arise/get up	sɔre
alert/warn	bɔ kɔkɔ	arithmetic	nkonta
alight	si fam(u)	arm	abasa
alike, be	sɛ	arrange	hyehyɛ
all	nyinaa	arrest	kye
allow	ma kwan	arrive	du
almighty	otumfoɔ	ashamed, be	ani wu
alone	nkõãã	ask	bisa
also	nso	assist	boa
always	bere biara/biaa	attempt/start	hyɛ aseɛ
ancestors	nananom	aunt	sewaa/
ancient times	tete / tetehɔ		maame
anger	abufuo	author	ɔtwerɛfoɔ
angry, be	bo fu	authority	tumi
animal	aboa	available, be	wɔ hɔ
ankle	nanpɔ so	awake	nyane
announce	(de/fa) to dwa	await	twɛn
	(make public)	aware, be	nim

131

B

baby	abofra/ akɔdaa ketewa	bless	hyira
		blind	ani afura
back	akyi(re)		(eyes are clothed)
bad, to be	nyɛ	blood	mogya
bake	tɔ	blow	hu
ban/forbid	bara	body	honam/hɔ̃
banana	kwadu	boil/cook	noa
baptise	bɔ asu	be boiling	huru
bargain	di ano	boil(s)	mpɔmpɔ
barrel	ankorɛ	book	buuku/nhoma
basket	kɛntɛn	booze	nom nsã
bat	ampan	borrow	fɛm
bath	dware	bother	ha (adwene)
bathroom	adwareɛ	bottle	toa
be	yɛ	bottom	aseɛ
beach	mpoano	box	adaka
bead(s)	ahweneɛ	boy	abarimowaa
beans	adua	brain	adwene
bear (fruits)	so	brassiere	bɔdis
beard	abɔdwesɛ	bread	paanoo
beast	aboa	break	bɔ (hollow objects)
beautiful	fɛ, fɛfɛ		
beauty	ahoɔfɛ	break	bu (straight objects)
become	yɛ		
bed	mpa	breasts	nufoɔ
beef	nantwinam	breathe	home
before	ansã na	bride	ayeforo
in front of	anim	bridegroom	ayefokunu
beg	srɛ/pa kyɛw	bright, be	hyerɛn
begin	hyɛ aseɛ	bring	fa bra/brɛ
believe	gye di	broad, be	trɛ
benefit	nya mfasoɔ	broom	praeɛ
bereaved, be	nya ayie	brother	nua barima
beware	hwɛ yiye	bucket	bokiti
big	kɛse	build	si (eg. dan)
be big	sõ / yɛ kɛse	burglary	krɔnoo
bind	kyekyere	burn	hye
bird	anomaa	bury	sie
birth, give	wo	business	adwuma
birth	awoɔ	buttocks	ɛtoɔ
bite	ka	buy	tɔ
black, be	biri	buy on credit	firi
blanket	kuntu		
bleed	mogya tu (blood gushes out)		

C

call (v)	frɛ	cockroach	tɛfrɛ
call (n)	(ɔ)frɛ	coconut	kube
calm, be	yɛ dinn / dwo	cocoyam	mankani
can/be able	tumi	cold	awɔ
cancel	twa mu	cold, be	awɔ de...
capture	kye(re)	collect	gyegye
care for	hwɛ ... so	comb	afɛɛ̃
career	adwuma	comb (hair)	nunu tirim
carry	sɔ̃/soa	combine	de/fa bɔ mu
cassava	bankye	command/tell	kã kyerɛ
catch	kye(re)	compare	fa to
cease	gyae		(put beside)
celebrate	di (plus noun eg.	come	bra (ba)
	awoda: birthday;	congratulate	ma mo! /
	buronya: X'mas)		ma tiri nkwã
cemetry	asieyɛ	congratulations	(wo) tiri nkwã
centre	mfinimfini	conscience	tiboa
certain, a	bi	consult	hũ / bisa
chair	akonnwa / adwa	continue	toa so
change (v)	sesã		(join to it)
change (n)	nsesã	cook (v)	noa
chapel	asɔredan	cool, be	dwo
character	suban	cough (v)	bɔ wa
charcoal	bidie	corpse	efunu
chat/converse	di nkɔmɔ	cost	ɛboɔ
cheap, be	yɛ fo	cottonwool	asaawa
cheeks	afono	count	kan
chest	koko	country	ɔman
chew	we /wesa	courage	akokuoduro
chicken (bird)	akokɔba	cow	nantwie
(meat)	akokɔnam	coward	ohũfoɔ
chief	ɔhene (M)	crab	kɔtɔ
	ɔhemaa (F)	crawl/creep	wea
child	ɛba	crocodile	dɛnkyɛm
	abofra/akɔdaa	cross (v)	twa
choose	yi (take out)	cruel, be	tirim yɛ sum
Christmas	buronya	cry (v)	sũ
church	asɔre	culture	amanneɛ
clever, be	nim adeɛ	cure (n)	ayaresa
climb	foro ˙	cure (v)	sa yareɛ
cloth	ntama/ntoma	curse	bɔ dua
close/shut	to m(u)	custom	amanneɛ
close, be	bɛn	cut (v)	twa
cock	akokɔnini	cut/sore	ekuro

133

D

daily	da biara	disappear	yera
damage	sɛe	discover	hũ
dance (v)	sa	discuss	kã hõ asɛm
dance (n)	asa		(talk about it)
dark, be	yɛ sum	disease	yareɛ
darkness	esum	disgrace (n)	animguaseɛ
'dash', give	to so	disgrace (v)	gu anim ase
'dash'	ntosoɔ	dislike	kyi
daughter	ba baa	disobedience	asoɔden
-in-law	aseɛ/asew	disobedient, be	yɛ asoɔden
dawn	anɔpa hema	distribute	kyekyɛ
deaf mute	emum	disturb	yɛ dede
death	owuo		(make noise)
debt	ɛka	divide	(kye)kyɛ mu
deceive	daadaa	(share out)	
deceit	nnaadaa	divorce (n)	awaregyaeɛ
decide	yɛ adwene	divorce (v)	gyae awareɛ
	(make mind up)	do	yɛ
		doctor	yaresafoɔ
decrease	te so	dog	ɔkraman
deep, be	(emu) dɔ	donate	kyɛ
delay	kyɛre	door	ɛpono
deliver	de/fa kɔ ma	dream (n)	daeɛ
deny	dane ano	dream (v)	sõ daeɛ
	(turn mouth)	dress	ataadeɛ
depart	kɔ	dress up	siesie hõ
descend	siane	drink (n)	nsã
describe	kã hõ asɛm	drink (v)	nom nsã
	(talk about it)	drive	kã kaa
desire	pɛ	drop (v)	tɔ fam(u)
dialect	kasa	drum (n)	twene
die	wu	drum (v)	bɔ twene
differ	sono	dry, be	wo
different, be	sono	dry (v)	hata
difficult	den, dennen	dust	mfuturo
dig	tu	duty	asɛdeɛ
direct / show	kyerɛ	dwell	te / tena

E

ear	asɔ̃	equal, be	yɛ pɛ
early	ntɛm	err	fom
earring(s)	asomuadeɛ	escape (v)	dwane
earth	asaase	evening	anwumerɛ
eat	di (with object)	every	biara / biaa
	didi (without obj.)	everybody	obiara
effort	mmɔden bɔ	everything	biribiara
egg(s)	(n)kosua	everywhere	baabiara
elder	ɔpanyin	evil	bɔne
elect/vote	to aba	examination	nsɔhwɛ
elephant	ɔsono	example	nhwɛsoɔ
encourage	hyɛ nkuran	exceed	boro so
energy	ahoɔden	exchange	sesã
enjoy/like	pɛ	expect	hwɛ anim
enough, be	sɔ̃	expectation	anidasoɔ
ensure	hwɛ ma (see to)	explain	kyerɛkyerɛ mu
enter	bra mu	extinguish	dum
entrust	de/fa hyɛ nsa	eye(s)	ani/aniwa
	(put into one's hand)	ball	ani kosua
envy (n)	anibereɛ	brow	ani ntɔn
envy (v)	ani bere adeɛ	lashes	anisua tɛtɛ

F

fabric	ntama/ntoma	fish	nsuom nam
face (n)	anim	flagrant, be	yɛ hwam
fade	hoa / pa	flat (adj)	tɛtrɛɛ
fall (n)	ahweaseɛ	flee	dwane
fall (v)	hwe ase	flesh	ɛnam
false, be	nyɛ nokorɛ	floor	ɛfam
	(not be true)	flour	esiam
falsehood	ntorɔ	flower	nhwiren
family	abusũã	fly (housefly)	nwansena
farm	afuo	fly (v)	tu
fat (n)	sradeɛ	fold (v)	bobɔ
fat, be	dɔre	follow	di akyi
father	agya / papa	folly	nkwaseasɛm
-in-law	aseɛ /asew	food	aduane
fear	suro	fool	kwasea
feather	takra	foolish, be	yɛ
feed	ma aduan		nkwaseasɛm
feel	te nkã	force	hyɛ

135

feet/foot	ɛnan	forehead	moma
festival	afahyɛ	forget	werɛ fi
fetish	ɔbosom	forgive	fa kyɛ
fight (n)	ɛkõ	fresh	mono/foforɔ
fight (v)	kõ	Friday	Efiada
fill	hyɛ ma	friend	adamfo
filth	ef ĩ	front	anim(u)
filthy	tan, tantan	frown	muna
find	hũ	fruit	duaba
finger(s)	nsatẽãã	fry	kye
finish (v)	wie	funeral	ayie
fire/firewood	egya	funny, be	yɛ sere
first, be	di kan	future	daakyẽ

G

game	agorɔ	gossip	kɔnkɔnsã/nsek
garden eggs	nyaadoa	govern	bu ɔman
gather	sesa/boaboa	government	amammuo
gentleman	krakye	Government	aban
get	nya	grandchild	nana
ghost	ɔsaman	grandparent	nana
gift	akyɛde	grasp / hold	som / sɔ mu
girl	abaayewa	great	kɛse
give	ma	green	ahaban mono
glad, be	ani gye	green	ahaban mono
go	kɔ	greet	kyea / kyia
goat	apɔnkye/abirekyie	grief	awerɛhoɔ/yea
God	Onyame/	grieve	di yea
	Onyankopɔn	grind	yam
	Twereduampɔn	ground	fam(u)
	Otumfoɔ	groundnuts	nkateɛ
gold	sika kɔkɔɔ	grow	nyin
good (n)	papa	grumble	nwiinwii
good (adj.)	pa/papa	guest	ɔhɔhoɔ

H

habit	suban	hoe	asɔ
hair	enwĩi	hold	som/sɔ mu
half	ɛfã	hole	tokuro/amona
hand	nsa	home	efie
hang	sɛn	homesick, be	fe fie
(washing)	hata	honest, be	kã nokorɛ
happen	si	honey	ɛwoɔ
happy, be	gye ani	hope (n)	anidasoɔ
hard	den	hope (v)	ani da so
harm	pira	horn	abɛn
hat	ɛkyɛ	horse	pɔnkɔ
hate	tan	hot	hye, hyehye
hatred	ɔtan	hour	dɔn
have	nya/wɔ	house	efie/ɛdan
head	eti(re)	housefly	nwansena
headache	atipaeɛ	housemaid	abaawa
heal	sa yare	how	sɛn
(be healed)	nya ahoɔden	hug	yɛ atuu
hear	te	huge, be	sõ/yɛ kɛse
heat	ɛhyeɛ	human being	onipa
heart	akoma	humble	dwo
heavy	du, duudu	humility	ahõ-brɛ-ase
heel	nantini	hunger	ɛkɔm
help (n)	mmoa	hungry, be	ɛkɔm de ...
help (v)	boa	hurry up	yɛ ntɛm
hide	sie	hurry, be in a	pɛ ntɛm
high, be	korɔn	hurt	pira
history	abakɔsɛm	husband	ekunu
hit	bo(ro) / bɔ		

I

idol	ɔbosom	insects (flies)	ntummoa
ill, be	yare	insult	di atɛm/yɛ
important	titiriw	intelligent, be	nim adeɛ
improve	yɛ yiye	interesting	anikã
in/inside	(e)mu	iron (n)	dadeɛ
include	kã hõ	iron (v)	to
increase (v)	yɛ kɛse	invalid	ɔyarefoɔ
injure	pira	issue	asɛm
insanity	abɔdam	ivory	ɔsono abɛn

J

jail	afiase	joke (n)	aseresɛm
jar	toa	joke (v)	di agorɔ
jaw	abɔdwe	judge (n)	ɔsennifoɔ
job	adwuma	judge (v)	di asɛm
join	toa so	jump	huri

K

kebab	kyinkyinga	king	ɔhene
keep/take	fa	kiss (v)	fe ano
keep safe	fa sie	kitchen	egyaade
kenkey	dɔkono	knee	kotodwe
kernel (palm)	adwe	knife	sekan
key	safoa	knock (v)	bɔ mu
kill	kũ/kum		

L

labour	adwumayɛ	leave	gya
lack/not have	ni	leg(s)	nan
ladder	atwereɛ	lend	fɛm
lady	awuraa	money	bɔ bosẽã
lag behind	ka akyire	length	tenten
lamb (meat)	dwanam	leopard	ɔsebɔ
lamp/lantern	kanea	let	ma
land	asaase	liar	ɔtorofo/
language	kasa		kohwini
large (be)	kɛse (sõ)	lie (n)	ɛtorɔ
lapse	pa hõ	lie (v)	di torɔ
last, be	we / di too	lie (down)	da
late, be	ka akyire	life	ɔbra
lather	ahuro	lift	ma so
laugh	sere	light (n)	hann
laughter	sereɛ	like (v)	pɛ
lavatory	tiafʼĩ	lime	ankaa twadeɛ
law	mmara	linguist/	ɔkyẽãme
lay	da	spokesman	
lay eggs	to kosua	lion	gyata
lead (v)	di kan/di anim	lip(s)	ano
leaf	ahahan/ahahan	listen	tie
leak	nwunu	little	ketewa/
learn	sũã		ketekete

little by little	nketenkete	lose	yera
live (v)	te	love (n)	ɔdɔ
lizard	koterɛ	fall in love	wu ma
long, be	ware		(die for)
long for	kɔn dɔ	love (v)	dɔ
look	hwɛ	lucky, be	ti yɛ
look for	hwehwɛ		

M

machine	afirie/afidie	mob	ɛdɔm
mad, be	bɔ dam	Monday	ɛdwoada
make	yɛ	money	sika
maid	abaawa	monkey	adoe/kwakuo
maize	aburoo	monster	kakaa
male/man	ɔbarima	month	bosome
mango	mango	moon	bosome
manioc	bankyɛ̃	morning	anɔpa
mankind	adasã	mosquito(es)	ntontom
march	bɔ nsra	mother	ɛna/maame
market	edwa	-in-law	aseɛ/asew
marriage	awareɛ	motherly	ɔbaatan
marry	ware	mountain	bepɔ
may	ebia	mourn / weep	sũ
meal	aduane	mouse	akura
mean	kyerɛ	mouth	ano/anom(u)
measure	susu	move	fi
meat	ɛnam	mud	nnɔteɛ
meet	hyia	murder (v)	kum / di awu
melt	nane	murder	awudie
mensturate	yɛ bra/bu nsa	murderer	owudifoɔ
middle	mfinimfini	mushroom	emmire
minute (time)	simma	music	nnwom
mirror	ahwehwɛ	must	ɛsɛ/ɛwɔ sɛ
miserable, be	werɛ ho		(it is necessary that)
mistake	mfomsoɔ	mutton	dwanam

N

nail	dadowa	neice/nephew	wɔfaase
name (n)	edin	new	foforɔ
name (v)	to din	next	nea edi so
call name	bɔ din	night	anadwo
nation	ɔman	no	daabi
navel	funuma	noise	dede
necessary, be	hĩa	nonsense	nkwaseasɛm
neck	ɛkɔn	nose	ɛhwene
necklace	kɔnmuade	not	(negative verb)
need	hĩa	notice/see	hũ
needle	paneɛ	now	seesei

O

oath	ntam	open/be open	bue
obey	di (mmara) so	opposite	hwɛ anim
	(keep to {rules})	orange(s)	ankaa
obtain	nya	orphan	agyanka/
odour	nkã		awisĩã
offer / give	de / fa ma	ought/must	ɛsɛ/ɛwɔ sɛ
often	taa	outside	akyi(re)
oil	anwã	over, be	wie
palm oil	ɛngo	overdo	yɛ boro so
coconut oil	kube-ngo	overlook	mfa nyɛ asɛm
old, be	nyini (to grow)		(not take seriously)
onion(s)	gyeene	overtake	pa hõ
only	nkõãã	owl	(ɔ)patuo

P

pack	hyehyɛ	patience	aboterɛ
page	kratafã	patient, be	si / nya aboterɛ
palm (tree)	abɛ	pause	gyina
palm (hand)	nsam(u)	pay	tua (ka)
pamper	korɔkorɔ	pawpaw	borɔferɛ
paper	krataa	peace	asomdwee
papaya	borɔferɛ	peanuts	nkateɛ
pardon	de / fa kyɛ	people	nnipa
parrot	ako	pepper	mako
pass	twa mu / sen	permit (v)	ma kwan
past, be	twa mu	person	onipa
pastor	ɔsɔfo	perspiration	fifire

perspire	fi fifire	pray	bɔ mpae
photograph	foto / mfoni	prayer	mpaeε
piano	sankuo	precede	di anim
pick	yi	pretend	boapa/hyε da
pig	prako	price	εboɔ
pillow	sumiε	prince/princess	ɔheneba
pineapple	aborɔbε	probe	hwε mu
pity	hũ mmɔbɔ	profit	nya mfasoɔ
plantain	borɔdeε	promise (n)	anohõba
ripe	kɔkɔɔ	promise (v)	bɔ anohõba
play	di agorɔ	promote	bɔ aba so
plead	pa kyεw		(pat on the shoulder)
plenty	pii		
pluck	te	proverb	εbε
pocket	bɔtɔ	give a proverb	bu bε
point/show	kyerε	proud, be	ma hõ so
poor, be	di hĩa		(raise one's self up)
poor person	ohĩani	public, make	fa to dwa
pork	prakonam	pull	twẽ
position	dibea	punish	twẽ asõ
pot	εsεn		(pull ear)
pour	hwie	pupil	sukuuni
poverty	ohĩa	put	de/fa to

Q

quarrel (n)	ntɔkwa /	question (n)	asεmmisa
	akasakasa	question (v)	bisa asεm
quarrel (v)	kõ	quick/quickly	ntεm
quarrelsome	pε ntɔkwa	quiet	dinn/komm
queen	ɔhemmaa	quit	gyae

R

race (run)	mmirika	receive	gye/nya
rain (n)	nsuo	recognise	hũ/kae
rain (v)	nsuo tɔ	recover	nya ahoɔden/
read	kan / kenkan		te apɔ
rear (animals)	yεn	red	kɔkɔɔ
reason	nea enti	red, be	bere
recall	kae	reduce	te so

141

reign (v)	di hene	reveal	yi kyerɛ/da adi
refund	san de/fa ma	ribs/rib cage	mfɛ̃
regret (v)	nu hõ	rice	ɛmo
relation/	busũãni	right (v. left)	nifã
relative		ring (n)	kawa/koa
relax	gye ahome	ring (bell)	bɔ dɔn
religion	nyamesom	ripe, be	bere
remain	ka	rise	sɔre
remember	kae	road	ɛkwan
remind	kae	roam	kyini
remit	mane	rob	wia
		room	ɛdan
remove	yi fi	rope	ahoma
repair (v)	siesie	round	kurukuruwa
repeat	kã bio	royal	ɔdehyeɛ
replace	hyɛ anan mu	rub	twitwi
reply	bua	rude, be	mmu adeɛ
return	san (bra)		(not respect)

S

sack (v)	yi adi	shadow	sunsum
sack (n)	bɔtɔ	shake	woso
sad, be	di awerɛhoɔ	share	kyɛ
salary	akatua	sheep	odwan
salt	nkyene	sheet (paper)	krataa
same	pɛ	bedsheet	mpasotam
sand	anwɛ̃ã	shine	hyerɛn
sandals	mpaboa	(of the sun)	(awia) bɔ
Saturday	Memeneda	shop / store	sotɔɔ / afiase
save (a life)	gye nkwã	shoulder	bati
say	kã	shout	tɛ̃ã mu
scarf	duku	show	kyerɛ
scatter	to petɛ̃	shy, be	fɛre
school	sukuu	sick, be	yare
scissors	apasoɔ	sieze/snatch	hwim
scratch	tĩ / tĩtĩ	silent	dinn, komm
scripture	anyamesɛm	sin (n)	bɔne
sea	ɛpo	sin (v)	yɛ bɔne
search/seek	hwehwɛ	sing	to nnwom
see	hwɛ / hũ	sir	owura
seem	te sɛ	sister	nua-baa
send (on errand)	soma	-in-law	akumaa
sensible, be	nim nyansã	sit (down)	tena (ase)
serve	som	sky	ewiem(u)/ɛso
sew	pam	slap	bɔ asom

slave/fellow	akoa	stand	gyina
sleep (n)	nna	stew	frɔeɛ
sleep (v)	da	stick (n)	abaa
sleepy, be	ani kom	stick (v)	tare
slow(ly)	brɛoo/bɔkɔɔ	stomach	yafunu / yam
small	ketewa	stone	ɛboɔ
small, be	sua	stool	asɛsɛdwa
smell (n)	nkǎ	stop	gyae
smell (v)	te nkǎ	story	asɛm
smile	nwenwene	fiction	anansesɛm
smoke (n)	wisie	straight	tɛɛ̌
snail	ɛnwa	strain (liquid)	sɔne
snake	ɔwɔ	strange	nwǒnwǎ
sneeze	nwansî	strength	ahoɔden
soft, be	go	strike / hit	bɔ
soil / earth	asaase	strong	den, dennen
son	ba barima	stubborn, be	asǒ yɛ den
-in-law	asɛɛ/asew	student	osũǎni
sorrow	awerɛhoɔ	study	sũǎ adeɛ
sorry, be	nu hǒ	succeed	di nkonim
soul	sunsum	success	nkonimdi
soup	nkwan	suck	fe
sow (v)	dua	sufficient, be	sǒ
speak	kasa	sugar	asikyire
speech	kasa	suit (v)	fata
spider	ananse	sun	awia
spinach	kontomire	Sunday	Kwasiada
spirit	honhom	surprise (v)	fu mu
spit	te ntasuo	surround	twa hyia
split	pae/dwa	swallow	mene
		swear	kǎ ntam
spoil	sɛe	sweat (n)	fifire
spokesman	ɔkyeame	sweat (v)	fi fifire
sponge	sapɔ	sweep	pra
spoon	atere	sweet	dɛ, dɛdɛ
spread	trɛ mu	swell	hono
squeeze	kyî mu	swim	dware asuo

143

T

table	ɛpon(o)	time	bere/ɛberɛ
tail	dua	timid, be	suro adeɛ
take	de (Stative)	tiny	ketekete(kete)
	fa (others)	title	abodin
talk	kasa	toilet	tiafi
tall	tenten	tongue	kɛtrɛma
tall, be	ware	tooth (teeth)	ɛsɛ̃
taste	kã hwɛ	top	ɛso
teach	kyerɛ (adeɛ)	tortoise	akyekyedeɛ
tear	te	touch	de/fa nsa kã
teeth	ɛsɛ̃	tough	(ani yɛ) den
tell	kã kyerɛ	town	kuro
tempt	sɔ hwɛ	trade (n)	adwadie
tend (do often)	taa yɛ	trade (v)	di dwa
test (n)	nsɔhwɛ	tradition	amanneɛ
test (v)	sɔ hwɛ	train (n)	keteke
testify	di adanseɛ	train (v)	tete
thank	da ase	translate	kyerɛ aseɛ
thanks	aseda	travel (n)	akwantuo
that (pronoun)	(ɛ)no	travel (v)	tu kwan
that (conj.)	sɛ	tread	tia
there	ɛhɔ	tree	dua
thaw	nane	trouble (n)	ɔhaw
thief	awi / krɔmfoɔ	trouble (v)	gyegye
thigh(s)	serɛ	true, be	yɛ nokorɛ
thing	adeɛ	trust	gye di
think	dwene	truth	nokorɛ
thirst	sukɔm	try	bɔ mmɔden
thirsty, be	sukɔm de	Tuesday	Benada
thread (n)	ahoma	turn	dane
thread (v)	sina	twin(s)	ata/ntaa
throat	mene		
throw (away)	to (twene)		
Thursday	Yawoada		

U

ugly	tan, tantan	upstairs	ɛsoro
ulcer	ekuro	urinate	dwonsɔ
uncle		urine	dwonsɔ
(maternal)	wɔfa	use	de/fa yɛ
(paternal)	agya /papa		(take do)
untie	sane	utensil	kyɛnsɛ̃ɛ̃

144

V

vacate	fi(ri)	visit (v)	sra
vacation, be on	ma kwan	vomit (n)	ɛfeɛ
vehicle	kaa	vomit (v)	fe
victory	nkunim	vote	to aba
village	akuraa	vulture	(ɔ)pɛtɛ
visit (n)	nsra		

W

wait	twɛn	who	hwan
wake	nyane	whole	nyinaa
walk	nante	why	adɛn
want	pɛ	wide	tɛtrɛɛ
war	ɛkõ	wide, be	trɛ
warn	bɔ kɔkɔ	widow (er)	kunafoɔ
wash (v)	si/horo	wife	yere
waste (v)	sɛe	win	di nkonim
watch (v)	wɛn	wind (n)	mframa
water	nsuo	window(s)	mpoma
way	ɛkwan	wipe	pepa
wear	fura /	wisdom	nyansã
	hyɛ	wise, be	hũ nyansã
weave	nwono	wish (n)	ɛpɛ
wed	hyia ayeforɔ	wish (v)	pɛ
wedding	ayefohyia/	witch	bayifoɔ
	ayeforɔ	witness (n)	dansedifoɔ
Wednesday	Wukuada	witness, bear	di adansee
weed	dɔ	woman	ɔbaa
weeds	ewura	wood	dua
week	nnaawɔtwe	word	asɛm
weep	sũ	world	wiase
well (n)	abura	worry (intr.)	dwennwen
wet, be	fɔ	(transitive)	ha / teetee
what	deɛn	wring	kyi mu
when	bere bɛn	wrist	abakɔn
where	ɛhẽ	write	twerɛ

Y

yam	bayerɛ	year	afe
yard/patio	adiwo	yearn	pɛ
yawn	heram	yes	aane

FOR FURTHER READING

Aboagye, J. Gyekye, 1984. *Wusum Borɔdeɛ a Sum Kwadu,* Bureau of Ghana Languages, Accra.

Amanfo, M. Boateng, 1990. *Mehunuiɛ a Anka,* Bureau of Ghana Languages, Accra.

Ankomah, P. Ɔ sene, 1968. *Ɛhɩa Wo a Nwu,* Bureau of Ghana Languages, Accra.

Benefo, Kofi, 1980. *Owuo Safoa,* Bureau of Ghana Languages, Accra.

Dolphyne, F. A., 1988. *The Akan (Twi-Fante) Language, Its Sound Systems and Tonal Structure,* Ghana Universities Press, Accra.

Manu, S.Y., 1992. *Mmɔfra Agorɔ,* Bureau of Ghana Languages, Accra.

Oduro, J., 1971. *Seanteɛ,* Presbyterian Book Depot Ltd., Accra.